Professional Exam

Paper C01

FUNDAMENTALS OF MANAGEMENT ACCOUNTING

CIMA EXAM PRACTICE KIT

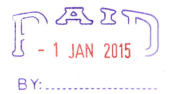

PAPER C01 : FUNDAMENTALS OF MANAGEMENT ACCOUNTING

Published by: Kaplan Publishing UK

Unit 2 The Business Centre, Molly Millars Lane, Wokingham, Berkshire RG41 2QZ

Copyright © 2013 Kaplan Financial Limited. All rights reserved.

No part of this publication may be reproduced, stored in a retrieval system or transmitted in any form or by any means electronic, mechanical, photocopying, recording or otherwise without the prior written permission of the publisher.

Acknowledgements

The CIMA Publishing trade mark is reproduced with kind permission of CIMA.

We are also grateful to CIMA for permission to reproduce past examination questions. The answers to CIMA Exams have been prepared by Kaplan Publishing, except in the case of the CIMA November 2010 and subsequent CIMA Exam answers where the official CIMA answers have been reproduced.

Notice

The text in this material and any others made available by any Kaplan Group company does not amount to advice on a particular matter and should not be taken as such. No reliance should be placed on the content as the basis for any investment or other decision or in connection with any advice given to third parties. Please consult your appropriate professional adviser as necessary. Kaplan Publishing Limited and all other Kaplan group companies expressly disclaim all liability to any person in respect of any losses or other claims, whether direct, indirect, incidental, consequential or otherwise arising in relation to the use of such materials.

British Library Cataloguing in Publication Data

A catalogue record for this book is available from the British Library

ISBN: 978-0-85732-962-2

Printed and bound in Great Britain.

CONTENTS

	Page
Syllabus Guidance, Learning Objectives and Verbs	v
Examination Techniques	xv
Present value table	xvii

Section

1	Practice questions	1
2	Objective test questions	21
3	Answers to practice questions	77
4	Answers to objective test questions	109
5	Mock Assessment 1	153
6	Mock Assessment 2	167
7	Answers to Mock Assessment 1	179
8	Answers to Mock Assessment 2	191

INDEX TO QUESTIONS AND ANSWERS

PRACTICE QUESTIONS

PAGE NUMBER

	QUESTION	ANSWER
THE CONTEXT OF MANAGEMENT ACCOUNTING	1	77
COST IDENTIFICATION AND BEHAVIOUR	2	79
OVERHEAD ANALYSIS	4	81
COST-VOLUME-PROFIT ANALYSIS	6	83
DECISION MAKING	7	84
INVESTMENT APPRAISAL	8	86
STANDARD COSTING AND VARIANCE ANALYSIS	8	87
BUDGETING	11	91
INTEGRATED ACCOUNTING SYSTEMS	14	96
COSTING SYSTEMS	16	101
PRESENTING MANAGEMENT INFORMATION	19	106

OBJECTIVE TEST QUESTIONS

PAGE NUMBER

	QUESTION	ANSWER
THE CONTEXT OF MANAGEMENT ACCOUNTING	21	109
COST IDENTIFICATION AND BEHAVIOUR	23	110
OVERHEAD ANALYSIS	29	113
COST-VOLUME-PROFIT ANALYSIS	35	118
DECISION MAKING	38	121
INVESTMENT APPRAISAL	42	124
STANDARD COSTING AND VARIANCE ANALYSIS	44	126
BUDGETING	51	133
INTEGRATED ACCOUNTING SYSTEMS	61	140
COSTING SYSTEMS	64	142
PRESENTING MANAGEMENT INFORMATION	73	150

SYLLABUS GUIDANCE, LEARNING OBJECTIVES AND VERBS

A THE CERTIFICATE IN BUSINESS ACCOUNTING

The Certificate introduces you to management accounting and gives you the basics of accounting and business. There are five subject areas, which are all tested by computer-based assessment (CBA). The five papers are:

- Fundamentals of Management Accounting
- Fundamentals of Financial Accounting
- Fundamentals of Business Mathematics
- Fundamentals of Business Economics
- Fundamentals of Ethics, Corporate Governance and Business Law

The Certificate is both a qualification in its own right and an entry route to the next stage in CIMA's examination structure.

The examination structure after the Certificate comprises:

- Managerial Level
- Strategic Level
- Test of Professional Competence in Management Accounting (an exam based on a case study).

This examination structure includes more advanced papers in Management Accounting. It is therefore very important that you work hard at Fundamentals of Management Accounting, not only because it is part of the Certificate, but also as a platform for more advanced studies. It is thus an important step in becoming a qualified member of the Chartered Institute of Management Accountants.

B AIMS OF THE SYLLABUS

The aims of the syllabus are

- to provide for the Institute, together with the practical experience requirements, an adequate basis for assuring society that those admitted to membership are competent to act as management accountants for entities, whether in manufacturing, commercial or service organisations, in the public or private sectors of the economy;
- to enable the Institute to examine whether prospective members have an adequate knowledge, understanding and mastery of the stated body of knowledge and skills;
- to complement the Institute's practical experience and skills development requirements.

PAPER C01 : FUNDAMENTALS OF MANAGEMENT ACCOUNTING

C STUDY WEIGHTINGS

A percentage weighting is shown against each topic in the syllabus. This is intended as a guide to the proportion of study time each topic requires.

All topics in the syllabus must be studied, since any single examination question may examine more than one topic, or carry a higher proportion of marks than the percentage study time suggested.

The weightings do not specify the number of marks that will be allocated to topics in the examination.

D LEARNING OUTCOMES

Each topic within the syllabus contains a list of learning outcomes, which should be read in conjunction with the knowledge content for the syllabus. A learning outcome has two main purposes:

1. to define the skill or ability that a well-prepared candidate should be able to exhibit in the examination;

2. to demonstrate the approach likely to be taken by examiners in examination questions.

The learning outcomes are part of a hierarchy of learning objectives. The verbs used at the beginning of each learning outcome relate to a specific learning objective, e.g. Evaluate alternative approaches to budgeting.

The verb 'evaluate' indicates a high-level learning objective. As learning objectives are hierarchical, it is expected that at this level students will have knowledge of different budgeting systems and methodologies and be able to apply them.

A list of the learning objectives and the verbs that appear in the syllabus learning outcomes and examinations follows.

Learning objectives	Verbs used	Definition
1 Knowledge		
What you are expected to know	List	Make a list of
	State	Express, fully or clearly, the details of/facts of
	Define	Give the exact meaning of
2 Comprehension		
What you are expected to understand	Describe	Communicate the key features of
	Distinguish	Highlight the differences between
	Explain	Make clear or intelligible/State the meaning of
	Identify	Recognise, establish or select after consideration
	Illustrate	Use an example to describe or explain something

SYLLABUS GUIDANCE, LEARNING OBJECTIVES AND VERBS

3	**Application**		
	How you are expected to apply your knowledge	Apply	To put to practical use
		Calculate/compute	To ascertain or reckon mathematically
		Demonstrate	To prove with certainty or to exhibit by practical means
		Prepare	To make or get ready for use
		Reconcile	To make or prove consistent/compatible
		Solve	Find an answer to
		Tabulate	Arrange in a table
4	**Analysis**		
	How you are expected to analyse the detail of what you have learned	Analyse	Examine in detail the structure of
		Categorise	Place into a defined class or division
		Compare and contrast	Show the similarities and/or differences between
		Construct	To build up or compile
		Discuss	To examine in detail by argument
		Interpret	To translate into intelligible or familiar terms
		Produce	To create or bring into existence
5	**Evaluation**	**Evaluation**	
	How you are expected to use your learning to evaluate, make decisions or recommendations	Advise	To counsel, inform or notify
		Evaluate	To appraise or assess the value of
		Recommend	To advise on a course of action

E COMPUTER-BASED ASSESSMENT

CIMA has introduced computer-based assessment (CBA) for all subjects at Certificate level. CIMA uses objective test questions in the computer-based assessment. The most common types are:

- multiple choice, where you have to choose the correct answer from a list of four possible answers. This could either be numbers or text.
- multiple choice with more choices and answers – for example, choosing two correct answers from a list of eight possible answers. This could either be numbers or text.
- single numeric entry, where you give your numeric answer e.g. profit is $10,000.
- multiple entry, where you give several numeric answers e.g. the charge for electricity is $2000 and the accrual is $200.
- true/false questions, where you state whether a statement is true or false e.g. external auditors report to the directors is FALSE.
- matching pairs of text e.g. the convention 'prudence' would be matched with the statement' inventories revalued at the lower of cost and net realisable value'.
- other types could be matching text with graphs and labelling graphs/diagrams.

In this Exam Practice Kit we have used these types of questions.

Some further guidance from CIMA on number entry questions is as follows:

- For number entry questions, you do not need to include currency symbols or other characters or symbols such as the percentage sign, as these will have been completed for you. You may use the decimal point but must not use any other characters when entering an answer (except numbers) so, for example, $10,500.80 would be input as 10500.80

- When expressing a decimal, for example a probability or correlation coefficient, you should include the leading zero (i.e. you should input 0.5 not .5)

- Negative numbers should be input using the minus sign, for example −1000

- You will receive an error message if you try to enter a character or symbol that is not permitted (for example a '£' or '%' sign)

- A small range of answers will normally be accepted, taking into account sensible rounding

Guidance re CIMA online calculator:

As part of the CIMA Certificate level computer based assessment software, candidates are now provided with a calculator. This calculator is onscreen and is available for the duration of the assessment. The calculator is available in each of the five Certificate level assessments and is accessed by clicking the calculator button in the top left hand corner of the screen at any time during the assessment.

All candidates must complete a 15 minute tutorial before the assessment begins and will have the opportunity to familiarise themselves with the calculator and practice using it.

Candidates may practise using the calculator by downloading and installing the practice exam at http://www.vue.com/athena/ . The calculator can be accessed from the fourth sample question (of 12).

Please note that the practice exam and tutorial provided by Pearson VUE at http://www.vue.com/athena/ is not specific to CIMA and includes the full range of question types the Pearson VUE software supports, some of which CIMA does not currently use.

F FUNDAMENTALS OF MANAGEMENT ACCOUNTING AND COMPUTER-BASED ASSESSMENT

The assessment for Fundamentals of Management Accounting is a two hour computer-based assessment comprising 50 compulsory questions, with one or more parts. CIMA is continuously developing the question styles within the CBA system and you are advised to try the online website demo at www.cimaglobal.com, to both gain familiarity with assessment software and examine the latest style of questions being used.

G SYLLABUS OUTLINE

Syllabus overview

This paper deals with the basic techniques for the identification and control of costs and cost management. It introduces the context of management accounting in commercial and public sector bodies and its wider role in society. It identifies the position of the management accountant within organisations and the role of CIMA.

Classification of costs and cost behaviour provides a basis for understanding the various tools available for planning, control and decision making. Budgetary control requires the setting of targets and standards while the analysis of variances demonstrates the levels of performance within organisations. Accounting control mechanisms are identified and applied to provide information to managers to achieve operational efficiency. Investment appraisal, break-even analysis and profit maximising are used to aid both long and short-term decision making.

Syllabus structure

The syllabus comprises the following topics and study weightings:

A	The context of management accounting	10%
B	Cost identification and behaviour	25%
C	Planning within organisations	30%
D	Accounting control systems	20%
E	Decision making	15%

PAPER C01 : FUNDAMENTALS OF MANAGEMENT ACCOUNTING

Learning outcomes and indicative syllabus content

C01 – A. THE CONTEXT OF MANAGEMENT ACCOUNTING (10%)

Learning outcomes
On completion of their studies students should be able to:

Lead	Component	Level	Indicative syllabus content
1. explain the purpose of management accounting	(a) define management accounting;	1	• The CIMA definition of management accounting. [1] • The IFAC definition of the domain of the professional accountant in business. [1] • Characteristics of financial information for operational, management and strategic levels within organisations. [1] • Cost object, concepts of target setting and responsibility accounting. [1] • Performance measurement and performance management using actual v budget comparisons, profitability and return on capital. [1] • Financial information requirements for companies, public bodies and society, including concepts of shareholder value, meeting society's needs and environmental costing. [1]
	(b) explain the importance of cost control and planning within organisations;	2	
	(c) describe how information can be used to identify performance within an organisation;	2	
	(d) explain the differences between financial information requirements for companies, public bodies and society.	2	
2. explain the role of the management accountant.	(a) explain the role of the management accountant and activities undertaken;	2	• The CIMA definition of the role of the management accountant. [1] • The IFAC definition of the role of the professional accountant in business. [1] • The nature of relationships between advisers and managers. [1] • The positioning of management accounting within the organisation. [1]
	(b) explain the relationship between the management accountant and the managers being served;	2	
	(c) explain the difference between placing management accounting within the finance function and a business partnering role within an organisation.	2	
3. explain the role of CIMA as a professional body for management accountants.	(a) explain the background to the formation of CIMA;	2	• The need for a professional body in management accounting – CIMA. [1] • CIMA's role in relation to its members, students, the profession of management accounting and society. [1]
	(b) explain the role of CIMA in developing the practice of management accounting	2	

C01 – B. COST IDENTIFICATION AND BEHAVIOUR (25%)

Learning outcomes
On completion of their studies students should be able to:

Lead	Component	Level	Indicative syllabus content
1. apply methods for identifying cost.	(a) explain the concept of a direct cost and an indirect cost;	2	• Classification of costs. [2] • The treatment of direct costs (specifically attributable to a cost object) and indirect costs (not specifically attributable) in ascertaining the cost of a 'cost object' e.g. a product, service, activity, customer. [2] • Cost measurement: historical versus economic costs. [2] • Overhead costs: allocation, apportionment, re-apportionment and absorption of overhead costs. *Note:* the repeated distribution method only will be used for reciprocal service department costs. [3] • Direct, variable and full costs of products, services and activities. [3] • Marginal cost pricing and full cost pricing to achieve specified return on sales or return on investment, mark-up and margins. *Note:* students are not expected to have a detailed knowledge of activity based costing (ABC). [3]
	(b) explain why the concept of 'cost' needs to be defined, in order to be meaningful;	2	
	(c) distinguish between the historical cost of an asset and the economic value of an asset to an organisation;	2	
	(d) prepare cost statements for allocation and apportionment of overheads, including reciprocal service departments;	3	
	(e) calculate direct, variable and full costs of products, services and activities using overhead absorption rates to trace indirect costs to cost units;	3	
	(f) apply cost information in pricing decisions.	3	
2. demonstrate cost behaviour.	(a) explain how costs behave as product, service or activity levels increase or decrease;	2	• Cost behaviour and activity levels. [2] • Fixed, variable and semi-variable costs. [2] • Step costs and the importance of timescale in analysing cost behaviour. [2] • High-low and graphical methods to establish fixed and variable elements of a semi-variable cost. *Note:* regression analysis is not required. [2]
	(b) distinguish between fixed, variable and semi-variable costs;	2	
	(c) explain step costs and the importance of timescales in their treatment as either variable or fixed;	2	
	(d) calculate the fixed and variable elements of a semi-variable cost.	3	

PAPER C01 : FUNDAMENTALS OF MANAGEMENT ACCOUNTING

C01 – C. PLANNING WITHIN ORGANISATIONS (30%)

Learning outcomes
On completion of their studies students should be able to:

Lead	Component	Level	Indicative syllabus content
1. prepare budgetary control statements.	(a) explain why organisations set out financial plans in the form of budgets, typically for a financial year;	2	• Budgeting for planning and control. [8] • Functional budgets including materials, labour and overheads; capital expenditure and depreciation budgets. [8] • Master budget, including income statement, statement of financial position and statement of cash flow. [8] • Reporting of actual outcomes against budget. [8] • Fixed and flexible budgeting. [8] • Budget variances. [8] • Interpretation and use of budget statements and budget variances. [8]
	(b) prepare functional budgets and budgets for capital expenditure and depreciation;	3	
	(c) prepare a master budget based on functional budgets;	3	
	(d) explain budget statements;	2	
	(e) identify the impact of budgeted cash surpluses and shortfalls on business operations;	2	
	(f) prepare a flexible budget;	3	
	(g) calculate budget variances;	3	
	(h) distinguish between fixed and flexible budgets;	2	
	(i) prepare a statement that reconciles budgeted contribution with actual contribution.	3	
2. prepare statements of variance analysis.	(a) explain the difference between ascertaining costs after the event and establishing standard costs in advance;	2	• Principles of standard costing. [7] • Preparation of standards for the variable elements of cost: material, labour, variable overhead. [7] • Variances: materials – total, price and usage; labour – total, rate and efficiency; variable overhead – total, expenditure and efficiency; sales – sales price and sales volume contribution. ***Note:*** students will be expected to calculate the sales volume contribution variance. [7] • Reconciliation of budget and actual contribution showing: variances for variable costs, sales prices and sales volumes, including possible inter-relations between cost variances, sales price and volume variances, and cost and sales variances. [7]
	(b) explain why planned standard costs, prices and volumes are useful in setting a benchmark;	2	
	(c) calculate standard costs for the material, labour and variable overhead elements of the cost of a product or service;	3	
	(d) calculate variances for materials, labour, variable overhead, sales prices and sales volumes;	3	
	(e) prepare a statement that reconciles budgeted contribution with actual contribution.	3	
	(f) prepare variance statements.	3	

C01 – D. ACCOUNTING CONTROL SYSTEMS (20%)

Learning outcomes
On completion of their studies students should be able to:

Lead	Component	Level	Indicative syllabus content
1. prepare integrated accounts in a costing environment.	(a) explain the principles of manufacturing accounts and the integration of the cost accounts with the financial accounting system;	2	• Manufacturing accounts including raw material, work in progress, finished goods and manufacturing overhead control accounts. [9] • Integrated ledgers including accounting for over and under absorption of production overhead. [9] • The treatment of variances as period entries in integrated ledger systems. [9] • Job, batch and process costing. *Note:* only the average cost method will be examined for process costing but students must be able to deal with differing degrees of completion of opening and closing stocks, normal losses and abnormal gains and losses, and the treatment of scrap value. [10]
	(b) prepare a set of integrated accounts, showing standard cost variances;	3	
	(c) explain job, batch, and process costing;	2	
	(d) prepare ledger accounts for job, batch and process costing systems.	3	
2. prepare financial statements for managers.	(a) prepare financial statements that inform management;	3	• Cost accounting statements for management information in production companies, service companies and not-for-profit organisations. Showing gross revenue, value-added, contribution, gross margin, marketing expense, general and administration expenses. [11]
	(b) distinguish between managerial reports in a range of organisations, including commercial enterprises, charities and public sector undertakings.	2	

PAPER C01: FUNDAMENTALS OF MANAGEMENT ACCOUNTING

C01 – E. DECISION MAKING (15%)

Learning outcomes
On completion of their studies students should be able to:

Lead	Component		Level	Indicative syllabus content
1. demonstrate the use of break-even analysis in making short-term decisions.	(a)	explain the contribution concept and its use in cost-volume-profit (CVP) analysis;	2	• Contribution concept and CVP analysis. [4] • Break-even charts, profit volume graphs, break-even point, profit target, margin of safety, contribution/sales ratio. [4]
	(b)	calculate the break-even point, profit target, margin of safety and profit/volume ratio for a single product or service;	3	
	(c)	prepare break-even charts and profit/volume graphs for a single product or service;	3	
2. apply basic approaches for use in decision making.	(a)	explain relevant costs and cash flows;	2	• Relevant costs and cash flows. [5] • Make or buy decisions. [5] • Limiting factor analysis for a multi-product company that has limited demand for each product and one other constraint or limiting factor. [5]
	(b)	explain make or buy decisions;	2	
	(c)	calculate the profit maximising product sales mix using limiting factor analysis.	3	
3. demonstrate the use of investment appraisal techniques in making long-term decisions.	(a)	explain the process of valuing long-term investments;	2	• Net present value, internal rate of return and payback methods. [6]
	(b)	calculate the net present value, internal rate of return and payback for an investment.	3	

EXAMINATION TECHNIQUES

COMPUTER-BASED ASSESSMENT

TEN GOLDEN RULES

1   Make sure you are familiar with the software before you start exam. You cannot speak to the invigilator once you have started.

2   These exam practice kits give you plenty of exam style questions to practise.

3   Attempt all questions, there is no negative marking.

4   Double check your answer before you put in the final answer.

5   On multiple choice questions (MCQs), there is only one correct answer.

6   Not all questions will be MCQs – you may have to fill in missing words or figures.

7   Identify the easy questions first and get some points on the board to build up your confidence.

8   Try and allow 15 minutes at the end to check your answers and make any corrections.

9   If you don't know the answer, try a process of elimination.

10 Work out your answer on paper first if it is easier for you. Scrap paper will be provided for you. You are allowed to take pens, pencils and rulers with you to the examination, but you are not allowed pencil cases, phones, paper or notes, or a calculator.

PRESENT VALUE TABLE

Present value of $1, that is $(1 + r)^{-n}$ where r = interest rate; n = number of periods until payment or receipt.

Periods (n)	Interest rates (r)									
	1%	2%	3%	4%	5%	5%	7%	8%	9%	10%
1	0.990	0.980	0.971	0.962	0.952	0.943	0.935	0.926	0.917	0.909
2	0.980	0.961	0.943	0.925	0.907	0.890	0.873	0.857	0.842	0.826
3	0.971	0.942	0.915	0.889	0.864	0.840	0.816	0.794	0.772	0.751
4	0.961	0.924	0.888	0.855	0.823	0.792	0.763	0.735	0.708	0.683
5	0.951	0.906	0.863	0.822	0.784	0.747	0.713	0.681	0.650	0.621
6	0.942	0.888	0.837	0.790	0.746	0.705	0.666	0.630	0.596	0.564
7	0.933	0.871	0.813	0.760	0.711	0.665	0.623	0.583	0.547	0.513
8	0.923	0.853	0.789	0.731	0.677	0.627	0.582	0.540	0.502	0.467
9	0.914	0.837	0.766	0.703	0.645	0.592	0.544	0.500	0.460	0.424
10	0.905	0.820	0.744	0.676	0.614	0.558	0.508	0.463	0.422	0.386
11	0.896	0.804	0.722	0.650	0.585	0.527	0.475	0.429	0.388	0.350
12	0.887	0.788	0.701	0.625	0.557	0.497	0.444	0.397	0.356	0.319
13	0.879	0.773	0.681	0.601	0.530	0.469	0.415	0.368	0.326	0.290
14	0.870	0.758	0.661	0.577	0.505	0.442	0.388	0.340	0.299	0.263
15	0.861	0.743	0.642	0.555	0.481	0.417	0.362	0.315	0.275	0.239
16	0.853	0.728	0.623	0.534	0.458	0.394	0.339	0.292	0.252	0.218
17	0.844	0.714	0.605	0.513	0.436	0.371	0.317	0.270	0.231	0.198
18	0.836	0.700	0.587	0.494	0.416	0.350	0.296	0.250	0.212	0.180
19	0.828	0.686	0.570	0.475	0.396	0.331	0.277	0.232	0.194	0.164
20	0.820	0.673	0.554	0.456	0.377	0.312	0.258	0.215	0.178	0.149

Periods (n)	Interest rates (r)									
	11%	12%	13%	14%	15%	16%	17%	18%	19%	20%
1	0.901	0.893	0.885	0.877	0.870	0.862	0.855	0.847	0.840	0.833
2	0.812	0.797	0.783	0.769	0.756	0.743	0.731	0.718	0.706	0.694
3	0.731	0.712	0.693	0.675	0.658	0.641	0.624	0.609	0.593	0.579
4	0.659	0.636	0.613	0.592	0.572	0.552	0.534	0.516	0.499	0.482
5	0.593	0.567	0.543	0.519	0.497	0.476	0.456	0.437	0.419	0.402
6	0.535	0.507	0.480	0.456	0.432	0.410	0.390	0.370	0.352	0.335
7	0.482	0.452	0.425	0.400	0.376	0.354	0.333	0.314	0.296	0.279
8	0.434	0.404	0.376	0.351	0.327	0.305	0.285	0.266	0.249	0.233
9	0.391	0.361	0.333	0.308	0.284	0.263	0.243	0.225	0.209	0.194
10	0.352	0.322	0.295	0.270	0.247	0.227	0.208	0.191	0.176	0.162
11	0.317	0.287	0.261	0.237	0.215	0.195	0.178	0.162	0.148	0.135
12	0.286	0.257	0.231	0.208	0.187	0.168	0.152	0.137	0.124	0.112
13	0.258	0.229	0.204	0.182	0.163	0.145	0.130	0.116	0.104	0.093
14	0.232	0.205	0.181	0.160	0.141	0.125	0.111	0.099	0.088	0.078
15	0.209	0.183	0.160	0.140	0.123	0.108	0.095	0.084	0.079	0.065
16	0.188	0.163	0.141	0.123	0.107	0.093	0.081	0.071	0.062	0.054
17	0.170	0.146	0.125	0.108	0.093	0.080	0.069	0.060	0.052	0.045
18	0.153	0.130	0.111	0.095	0.081	0.069	0.059	0.051	0.044	0.038
19	0.138	0.116	0.098	0.083	0.070	0.060	0.051	0.043	0.037	0.031
20	0.124	0.104	0.087	0.073	0.061	0.051	0.043	0.037	0.031	0.026

Cumulative present value of $1 per annum, Receivable or Payable at the end of each year for n years $\quad \frac{1-(1+r)^{-n}}{r}$

Periods (n)	Interest rates (r)									
	1%	2%	3%	4%	5%	6%	7%	8%	9%	10%
1	0.990	0.980	0.971	0.962	0.952	0.943	0.935	0.926	0.917	0.909
2	1.970	1.942	1.913	1.886	1.859	1.833	1.808	1.783	1.759	1.736
3	2.941	2.884	2.829	2.775	2.723	2.673	2.624	2.577	2.531	2.487
4	3.902	3.808	3.717	3.630	3.546	3.465	3.387	3.312	3.240	3.170
5	4.853	4.713	4.580	4.452	4.329	4.212	4.100	3.993	3.890	3.791
6	5.795	5.601	5.417	5.242	5.076	4.917	4.767	4.623	4.486	4.355
7	6.728	6.472	6.230	6.002	5.786	5.582	5.389	5.206	5.033	4.868
8	7.652	7.325	7.020	6.733	6.463	6.210	5.971	5.747	5.535	5.335
9	8.566	8.162	7.786	7.435	7.108	6.802	6.515	6.247	5.995	5.759
10	9.471	8.983	8.530	8.111	7.722	7.360	7.024	6.710	6.418	6.145
11	10.368	9.787	9.253	8.760	8.306	7.887	7.499	7.139	6.805	6.495
12	11.255	10.575	9.954	9.385	8.863	8.384	7.943	7.536	7.161	6.814
13	12.134	11.348	10.635	9.986	9.394	8.853	8.358	7.904	7.487	7.103
14	13.004	12.106	11.296	10.563	9.899	9.295	8.745	8.244	7.786	7.367
15	13.865	12.849	11.938	11.118	10.380	9.712	9.108	8.559	8.061	7.606
16	14.718	13.578	12.561	11.652	10.838	10.106	9.447	8.851	8.313	7.824
17	15.562	14.292	13.166	12.166	11.274	10.477	9.763	9.122	8.544	8.022
18	16.398	14.992	13.754	12.659	11.690	10.828	10.059	9.372	8.756	8.201
19	17.226	15.679	14.324	13.134	12.085	11.158	10.336	9.604	8.950	8.365
20	18.046	16.351	14.878	13.590	12.462	11.470	10.594	9.818	9.129	8.514

Periods (n)	Interest rates (r)									
	11%	12%	13%	14%	15%	16%	17%	18%	19%	20%
1	0.901	0.893	0.885	0.877	0.870	0.862	0.855	0.847	0.840	0.833
2	1.713	1.690	1.668	1.647	1.626	1.605	1.585	1.566	1.547	1.528
3	2.444	2.402	2.361	2.322	2.283	2.246	2.210	2.174	2.140	2.106
4	3.102	3.037	2.974	2.914	2.855	2.798	2.743	2.690	2.639	2.589
5	3.696	3.605	3.517	3.433	3.352	3.274	3.199	3.127	3.058	2.991
6	4.231	4.111	3.998	3.889	3.784	3.685	3.589	3.498	3.410	3.326
7	4.712	4.564	4.423	4.288	4.160	4.039	3.922	3.812	3.706	3.605
8	5.146	4.968	4.799	4.639	4.487	4.344	4.207	4.078	3.954	3.837
9	5.537	5.328	5.132	4.946	4.772	4.607	4.451	4.303	4.163	4.031
10	5.889	5.650	5.426	5.216	5.019	4.833	4.659	4.494	4.339	4.192
11	6.207	5.938	5.687	5.453	5.234	5.029	4.836	4.656	4.486	4.327
12	6.492	6.194	5.918	5.660	5.421	5.197	4.988	7.793	4.611	4.439
13	6.750	6.424	6.122	5.842	5.583	5.342	5.118	4.910	4.715	4.533
14	6.982	6.628	6.302	6.002	5.724	5.468	5.229	5.008	4.802	4.611
15	7.191	6.811	6.462	6.142	5.847	5.575	5.324	5.092	4.876	4.675
16	7.379	6.974	6.604	6.265	5.954	5.668	5.405	5.162	4.938	4.730
17	7.549	7.120	6.729	6.373	6.047	5.749	5.475	5.222	4.990	4.775
18	7.702	7.250	6.840	6.467	6.128	5.818	5.534	5.273	5.033	4.812
19	7.839	7.366	6.938	6.550	6.198	5.877	5.584	5.316	5.070	4.843
20	7.963	7.469	7.025	6.623	6.259	5.929	5.628	5.353	5.101	4.870

Section 1

PRACTICE QUESTIONS

THE CONTEXT OF MANAGEMENT ACCOUNTING

1   Explain the difference between management and financial accounting.

2   List the three main purposes of management accounting.

3   Explain the three levels at which planning is undertaken within an organisation.

4   List the eight characteristics of good information.

5   Explain the difference between the detail of information produced for use at the strategic level to that produced for use at the operational level.

6   Explain the advantages of setting up a shared services centre over positioning the management accountant within the business as a dedicated business partner.

7   List the five fundamental principles of the CIMA code of ethics.

8   Explain the disadvantages of setting up the finance function using business process outsourcing.

9   Explain the purpose of the CGMA designation.

10   Give three examples of internal environmental costs.

COST IDENTIFICATION AND BEHAVIOUR

11 Define the following:

    (a)   Cost unit

    (b)   Cost centre

    (c)   Cost object

12 Explain the three main ways in which costs may be classified.

13 Define a direct cost and an indirect cost. Give an example of each for a book publisher.

14 Define prime cost.

15 Match a graph to each of the following costs:

    (a)   Variable cost per unit

    (b)   Total fixed cost

    (c)   Stepped fixed costs

    (d)   Total variable cost

    (e)   Semi-variable cost

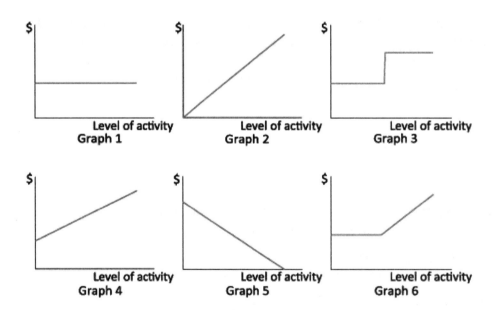

16 Define a semi-variable cost and explain how this type of cost changes in relation to changes in the level of activity.

PRACTICE QUESTIONS : SECTION 1

17 A company has recorded the following data for a semi-variable cost:

Activity level	Total cost $
1,800	35,250
2,200	39,500
1,500	30,000
2,500	41,500
2,800	43,000

Using the high-low method, calculate the fixed cost, the variable cost per unit and estimate the total cost for an activity level of 3,000.

18 Explain what is meant by marginal costing.

19 Define an overhead cost.

20 State six different benefits of cost accounting.

(i)

(ii)

(iii)

(iv)

(v)

(vi)

21 Complete the following statements.

(i) A _____ is a unit of product or service in relation to which costs are ascertained.

(ii) A _____ cost is an expenditure which can be economically identified with and specifically measured in respect to a relevant cost object.

(iii) _____ cost is the total cost of direct material, direct labour and direct expenses.

(iv) An _____ or _____ cost is an expenditure on labour, materials or services which cannot be economically identified with a specific saleable cost unit.

(v) A cost _____ is a production or service location, function, activity or item of equipment for which costs are accumulated.

(vi) A _____ cost is a cost which is incurred for an accounting period and which tends to be unaffected by fluctuations in the levels of activity.

(vii) A _____ cost is a cost which changes in total in relation to the level of output.

(viii) An example of a fixed cost is _____.

(ix) An example of a variable cost is _____.

(x) An example of a semi-fixed/semi-variable cost is _____.

22 The relationship between total costs Y and activity X is in the form:

Y = a + bX

a =

b =

PAPER C01 : FUNDAMENTALS OF MANAGEMENT ACCOUNTING

23 Use the high–low method to calculate the fixed and variable elements of the following costs.

	Units	Cost
July	400	$1,000
August	500	$1,200
September	600	$1,400
October	700	$1,600
November	800	$1,800
December	900	$2,000

24 The variable production cost per unit of product B is $2 and the fixed production overhead is $4,000. The total production cost of producing 3,000 units of B in a period is $_____.

25 Describe the scattergraph method of analysing a semi-variable cost into its fixed and variable elements.

26 What is a step cost and give an example of one?

OVERHEAD ANALYSIS

27 By what basis would you apportion the following cost?

(i)   Rent

(ii) Power

(iii) Depreciation

(iv) Cost of canteen facility

(v)   Machine maintenance labour

(vi) Supervision

28 A company occupies 100,000 sq. metres with an annual rent of $500,000. Department A takes up 30,000 sq. metres, Department B uses 20,000 sq. metres and Department C and D use 25,000 sq. metres each. How much rent should be apportioned to Department A?

29 State five methods by which overheads can be absorbed into cost units.

(i)

(ii)

(iii)

(iv)

(v)

PRACTICE QUESTIONS : SECTION 1

Questions 30–32 are based on the following information:

A manufacturing company uses pre-determined rates for absorbing overheads based on the budgeted level of activity. A rate of $22 per labour hour has been calculated for the Assembly Department for which the following overhead expenditures at various activity levels have been estimated.

Assembly department total overheads $	Number of labour hours
338,875	14,500
347,625	15,500
356,375	16,500

30 Calculate (i) the variable overhead absorption rate per labour hour and (ii) the estimated total fixed overheads.

31 Calculate the budgeted level of activity in labour hours.

32 Calculate the amount of under/over absorption of overheads, if the actual labour hours were 15,850 and actual overheads were $355,050.

33 Define the following.

(a) overhead absorption

(b) overhead apportionment

(c) overhead allocation

34 Explain reciprocal servicing.

35 Explain how a predetermined overhead absorption rate is calculated.

36 Explain why an under- or over-absorption of overhead may occur.

37 A company has two production cost centres (A and B) and two service cost centres (C and D). The overhead costs after the initial allocation of overheads is given below.

Service cost centres C and D use each other's facilities in the proportions shown.

Using the repeated distribution method, calculate the total overhead charge for the two production departments.

	Production A	Production B	Service C	Service D
Total overheads ($)	10,000	25,000	21,000	15,000
Use of Service C	45%	45%		10%
Use of Service D	35%	60%	5%	

PAPER C01 : FUNDAMENTALS OF MANAGEMENT ACCOUNTING

COST-VOLUME-PROFIT ANALYSIS

38 What is contribution?

39 Break-even analysis

Consider the following data:

Selling price	$10 per unit
Variable cost	$6 per unit
Fixed costs	$1,000

How many units need to be sold to break even?

40 Using the same data as in Question 39, if fixed costs rise by 20% and the company need to make a profit of $350, how many units need to be sold?

41 If budgeted production and sales are 80,000 units and selling price is $10, variable cost is $5 per unit and fixed costs are $200,000, calculate the margin of safety.

42 A product has an operating statement for the sales of 1,000 units.

	$
Sales	10,000
Variable costs	6,000
Fixed costs	2,500

You are required to calculate:

(i) Profitability to sales

(ii) Contribution to sales

(iii) Break-even sales in

(1) value

(2) units

(iv) Margin of safety

43 What is the difference between a break-even chart and a profit-volume chart?

44 Why does an economist's break-even chart differ from that of an accountant?

DECISION MAKING

RELEVANT COST

45 List three features of relevant costs and revenues.

46 List six examples of non-relevant costs.

47 Explain the concept of opportunity costs.

LIMITING FACTOR ANALYSIS AND MAKE OR BUY DECISIONS

48 A company makes two products which both use the same type and grade of materials and labour but in different quantities.

	Product A	Product B
Labour hours	5	8
Materials/unit	$20	$15

During each week there are 2,000 labour hours available and the value of material available is limited to $12,000.

Product A makes a contribution of $5 per unit and product B earns $6 contribution per unit.

Which product should they make?

49 What is a limiting factor?

50 A company makes three products X, Y and Z. All three products use the same type of labour which is limited to 1,000 hours per month. Individual details are as follows:

Product	X	Y	Z
Contribution/unit	$25	$40	$32
Labour hours/unit	5	6	8
Maximum demand	50	100	400

What quantities of each product should they produce?

PAPER C01 : FUNDAMENTALS OF MANAGEMENT ACCOUNTING

INVESTMENT APPRAISAL

51 Explain the advantages and disadvantages of the payback method of investment appraisal.

52 Explain the advantages and disadvantages of the NPV method of investment appraisal.

53 A project requires an initial investment of $190,000. The company has a cost of capital of 10%. The following cash flows have been estimated for the life of the project:

Year	Cash flow
1	$54,000
2	$68,000
3	$87,000
4	$45,000

Calculate the IRR of the project and recommend whether the project should be undertaken.

54 Explain the time value of money and how this is dealt with in investment appraisal.

STANDARD COSTING AND VARIANCE ANALYSIS

55 What is standard costing?

56 What is a standard cost?

57 Distinguish between four types of standard.

(i)

(ii)

(iii)

(iv)

58 Write down the four cost elements for a standard cost.

(i)

(ii)

(iii)

(iv)

59 What is a standard hour?

PRACTICE QUESTIONS : SECTION 1

60 A factory had an activity level of 110% with the following output.

	Units	Standard minutes each
Product A	5,000	5
Product B	2,500	10
Product C	3,000	15

The budgeted direct labour cost was $5,000

Calculate:

(i) The budgeted standard hours

(ii) Budgeted labour cost per standard hour

61 Annie's cafe makes sandwiches for sale. Contents of their cheese and pickle sandwich are as follows:

2 slices of bread

50 g of cheese

25 g of pickle

5 g of butter

Losses due to accidental damage are estimated to be 5% of the materials input. Materials can be bought from the cash and carry at the following prices:

Bread $0.50 per loaf of 20 slices

Cheese $3 per kg

Pickle $2 per kg

Butter $1.50 per kg

Prepare the standard cost of one cheese and pickle sandwich.

62 Give five possible sources of information from which a standard materials price may be estimated.

(i)

(ii)

(iii)

(iv)

(v)

63 Standard raw materials consist of

5 kg A at $2 per kg

3 kg B at $3 per kg

Standard labour consists of

4 hours grade X at $5 per hour

5 hours grade Y at $10 per hour

Standard variable overheads are charged at $20 per hour

Prepare a standard cost card extract to show the standard variable cost.

64 In setting standards, three things should be kept in mind. They are

(i)

(ii)

(iii)

65 What is a cost variance?

66 What would an adverse materials price variance and a favourable materials usage variance indicate and what might this be caused by?

67 What does an adverse variable overhead efficiency variance indicate and what might be the cause?

68 What is the relationship between the labour efficiency variance and the variable overhead efficiency variance? Why might the monetary value be different?

69 Sales variances

Budgeted sales	500 units
Actual sales	480 units
Budgeted selling price	$100
Actual selling price	$110
Variable cost per unit	$50
Fixed cost per unit	$15

Calculate

(i) Sales price variance

(ii) Sales volume contribution variance

PRACTICE QUESTIONS : SECTION 1

70 Labour variances

Actual production	700 units
Standard wage	$4 per hour
Standard time allowed per unit	1.5 hours
Actual hours worked	1,000 hours
Actual wages paid	$4200

Calculate

(i) Labour rate variance.

(ii) Labour efficiency variance.

71 Materials variances

Standard cost 2 kg at	$10 per kg
Actual output	1,000 units
Materials purchased and used	2250 kg
Material cost	$20,500

Calculate

(i) Material price variance.

(ii) Material usage variance.

72 Explain briefly the possible causes of

(i) The material usage variance;

(ii) The labour rate variance;

(iii) The sales volume contribution variance.

73 Explain the meaning and relevance of interdependence of variances when reporting to managers.

BUDGETING

74 State six aims of budgeting.

(i)

(ii)

(iii)

(iv)

(v)

(vi)

75 What is a budget?

76 State seven items that might be included in a budget manual.

(i)

(ii)

(iii)

(iv)

(v)

(vi)

77 The production budget needs to be translated into requirements for:

(i)

(ii)

(iii)

(iv)

78 What is a budget centre?

79 What is the difference between a budget and a forecast?

80 Consider the following budgeted figures:

Sales	$450,000
Opening inventory	$20,000
Closing inventory	$30,000
Raw materials	$120,000
Direct labour	$130,000
Production overhead	$120,000
Administration	$45,000

What is the budgeted operating profit for the period?

81 Name six types of functional budgets.

(i)

(ii)

(iii)

(iv)

(v)

(vi)

82 What is the principal budget factor?

83 What is a cash budget?

PRACTICE QUESTIONS : SECTION 1

84 What are the objectives of a cash budget?

85 The budgeted sales for a company during the first three months of next year are as follows:

	January	February	March
	$	$	$
Sales	500	600	800

All sales are on credit, and customers tend to pay as follows:

	%
In month of sale	10
In month after sale	40
Two months after sale	45

Bad debt is 5% of sales. How much cash is collected in March?

Questions 86–88 are based on the following budgeted data:

	January	February	March
	Units	Units	Units
Opening inventory	100	150	120
Closing inventory	150	120	180
Sales	400	450	420

The cost of inventory is $5 per unit and 50% of purchases are paid in cash and 50% are paid on credit, two months after the purchase.

86 Calculate the budgeted purchases in units for February.

87 How many units were budgeted to be purchased over the three-month period?

88 How much was budgeted to be paid to suppliers during March?

89 What is a flexible budget?

90 State two advantages and two disadvantages of a flexible budget.

91 What is a volume variance?

92 What is an expenditure variance?

93 What is a flexed budget?

INTEGRATED ACCOUNTING SYSTEMS

94 What are integrated accounts?

Questions 95–96 are based on the following information:

NB Ltd operates an integrated accounting system. At the beginning of October, the following balances appeared in the trial balance:

	$000	$000	$000
Freehold buildings		800	
Plant and equipment, at cost		480	
Provision for depreciation on plant and equipment			100
Inventories:			
Raw materials		400	
Work-in-process 1:			
Direct materials	71		
Direct wages	50		
Production overhead	125	246	
Work-in-process 2:			
Direct materials	127		
Direct wages	70		
Production overhead	105	302	
Finished goods		60	
Receivables		1,120	
Capital			2,200
Profit retained			220
Payables			300
Bank			464
Sales			1,200
Cost of sales		888	
Abnormal loss		9	
Production overhead under/over absorbed			21
Administration overhead		120	
Selling and distribution overhead		80	
		4,505	4,505

The transactions during the month of October were

	$000
Raw materials purchased on credit	210
Raw materials returned to suppliers	10
Raw materials issued to	
Process 1	136
Process 2	44
Direct wages incurred	
Process 1	84
Process 2	130
Direct wages paid	200
Production salaries paid	170
Production expenses paid	250
Received from customers	1,140
Paid to suppliers	330
Administration overhead paid	108
Selling and distribution overhead paid	84
Sales on credit	1,100
Cost of goods sold	844

	Direct materials $000	Direct wages $000
Abnormal loss		
Process 1	6	4
Process 2	18	6
Transfer from process 1 to process 2	154	94
Transfer from process 2 to finished goods	558	140

Plant and equipment is depreciated at the rate of 20% per annum, using the straight-line basis. Production overhead is absorbed on the basis of direct wages cost.

95 What are the production overhead absorption rates for process 1 and for process 2?

96 Write up the ledger accounts.

97 A company operates an integrated cost and financial accounting system. If an issue of direct materials to production was requisitioned what would the accounting entries be?

98 State six accounts in a manufacturing business which will contain control accounts.

COSTING SYSTEMS

JOB AND BATCH COSTING

99 What is job costing?

100 State four items which would appear on a job cost sheet:

(i)

(ii)

(iii)

(iv)

101 What is batch costing?

102 When products are made in batches for inventory, the quantity to be produced will be determined by:

(i)

(ii)

(iii)

(iv)

103 Company A bases its estimates on the following formula:

Total cost = Prime cost + 40% overhead

Selling price = Total cost + 25% profit

Estimates for two jobs show

	Job X	Job Y
	$	$
Direct materials	200	100
Direct wages $5 per hour	500	600
Prime cost	700	700

Calculate the selling price of each job. Is this the best way to absorb overhead?

104 State three discrepancies which could appear between a job cost card and the financial accounts:

(i)

(ii)

(iii)

PRACTICE QUESTIONS : **SECTION 1**

Questions 105–107 are based on the following information:

A company specialises in printing advertising leaflets and is in the process of preparing its price list. The most popular requirement is for a folded leaflet made from a single sheet of A4 paper. From past records and budgeted figures, the following data have been estimated for a typical batch of 10,000 leaflets.

Artwork $65

Machine setting 4 hours at $22 per hour

Paper $12.50 per 1,000 sheets

Ink and consumables $40

Printers' wages 4 hours at $8 per hour

General fixed overheads are $15,000 per period during which a total of 600 labour hours are expected to be worked.

The firm wishes to achieve 30% profit on sales.

105 Calculate the selling price per thousand leaflets for quantities of 10,000 and 20,000 leaflets.

106 Calculate the profit for the period if 64 batches of 10,000 and 36 batches of 20,000 were sold and costs and revenues were as budgeted.

107 Comment on the results achieved in the period.

108 What is the collective term for job AND batch costing and what are their distinguishing features?

PROCESS COSTING

109 What is process costing and when is it applied?

110 What is a normal loss?

111 Calculate the cost per tonne from the following data:

	$
Input 5,000 tonnes	20,000
Labour cost	8,000
Overhead	5,000

Normal loss is 10% of input and has a scrap value of $3 per tonne.

Write up the process account and the normal loss account.

112 Distinguish between an abnormal loss and an abnormal gain.

PAPER C01 : FUNDAMENTALS OF MANAGEMENT ACCOUNTING

113 Calculate the net cost/profit of the abnormal loss/gain from the following data:

Input quantity	5,000 kg at $5 per kg
Normal loss	10%
Process costs	$17,490
Actual output	4,200 kg

Losses are sold for $2 per kg.

114 A manufacturer starts a process on 1st January. In the month of January, he starts work on 20,000 units of production. At the end of the month there are 5,000 units still in process which are 75% complete. Costs for the period were $20,625.

Calculate:

(i) The value of completed units at the end of January

(ii) The value of WIP at the end of January

Questions 115–117 are based on the following information:

C Ltd manufactures a range of products and the data below refer to one product which goes through one process only. The company operates a 13 four-weekly reporting system for process and product costs and the data given below relate to Period 10.

There was no opening work in progress.

5,000 units of materials input at $2.94 per unit entered the process.

	$
Further direct materials added	13,830
Direct wages incurred	6,555
Production overhead	7,470

Normal loss is 3% of input.

Closing WIP was 800 units but these were incomplete, having reached the following percentages of completion for each of the elements of cost listed:

	%
Direct materials added	75
Direct wages	50
Production overhead	25

270 units were scrapped after a quality control check when the units were at the following degrees of completion.

	%
Direct materials added	66⅔
Direct wages	33⅓
Production overhead	16⅔

Units scrapped, regardless of the degree of completion, are sold for $1 each and it is company policy to credit the process account with the scrap value of normal loss units.

PRACTICE QUESTIONS : SECTION 1

115 Prepare the Period 10 process account.

116 Prepare the abnormal gain or loss account.

117 Suggest two causes of

(i) Abnormal loss

(ii) Abnormal gain

PRESENTING MANAGEMENT INFORMATION

118 What is service costing?

119 State three industries where service costing can be applied.

(i)

(ii)

(iii)

120 Cost units for service industries

Match the following cost units with the following services:

Service	Cost unit
Restaurants	Passenger miles
Carriers	Patient days
Hospitals	Tonne-miles
Passenger transport	Meals served

121 State four differences between a service industry and a manufacturing industry.

(i)

(ii)

(iii)

(iv)

122 State three differences between a manufacturing and a service cost statement.

(i)

(ii)

(iii)

123 What is a composite cost unit?

PAPER C01 : FUNDAMENTALS OF MANAGEMENT ACCOUNTING

Questions 124–127 are based on the following scenario:

George and Helen have recently set up their own auditing practice. They have agreed to take a salary of $20,000 per annum in their first year of trading. They have purchased two cars at $13,000 each and expect to use them for three years. At the end of three years, the cars have an expected resale value of $4,000. Straight line depreciation is to be used.

Each expects to work for 8 hours per day, 5 days per week and for 45 weeks per year. They refer to this as available time.

Around 25% of available time is expected to be dealing with administration matters related to their own business and in the first year there will be an idle time of 22.5% of available time. The remainder of available time is expected to be charged to clients.

They agree that their fees should be based on:

(i)   An hourly rate for productive client work

(ii) An hourly rate for travelling to/from clients

(iii) Rate per mile travelled to/from clients

They expect that the travelling time will equal 25% of their chargeable time and will cover 18,000 miles.

This time should be charged at 1/3 of their hourly rate. Other costs include

	$
Electricity	1,200
Fuel for vehicles	1,800
Insurance – office	600
Insurance – vehicles	800
Mobile telephone	1,200
Office rent and rates	8,400
Office telephone	1,800
Postage	500
Secretarial costs	8,400
Vehicle repairs	1,200
Vehicle road tax	280

124 The hourly rate for client work was $

125 The hourly rate for travelling to/from clients was $

126 The rate per mile travelled to/from clients was $

127 What method of cost accounting was used in the last three examples?

Section 2

OBJECTIVE TEST QUESTIONS

THE CONTEXT OF MANAGEMENT ACCOUNTING

1   Which of the following is a disadvantage of Business Process Outsourcing?

   A   Higher cost

   B   Less specialism

   C   Loss of control

   D   Loss of economies of scale

2   **Consider the following reports**

   (i)   Cash Budget

   (ii)   Cash flow statement

   (iii) Variance report

   (iv)   Income statement

   Which of the above would generally be produced by a management accountant?

   A   (i) and (ii) only

   B   (ii) and (iv) only

   C   (i), (ii) and (iii) only

   D   (i) and (iii) only

3   **Do the comments relate to management or financial accounting?**

	Management accounting	*Financial accounting*
Uses historical data		
Is carried out at the discretion of management		
Uses non financial information		
Aids planning within the organisation		

PAPER C01 : FUNDAMENTALS OF MANAGEMENT ACCOUNTING

4 **Management information is used at different levels of the organisation**

(i) Information used by strategic management tends to be summarised

(ii) Information used by strategic management tends to be forward looking

(iii) information used by operational management tends to contain estimates

(iv) information used by operational management tends to be required frequently

Which of the above statements are true?

A (i), (ii) and (iv) only

B (i), (iii) and (iv) only

C (ii) and (iii) only

D (iii) and (iv) only

5 **Which of the following is not a role of management accounting, as defined by CIMA?**

A Design reward strategies for executives and shareholders

B Measure and report financial and non-financial performance to management and other stakeholders

C Check the accuracy of the financial statements produced by the organisation

D Implement corporate governance procedures, risk management and internal control

6 **Management accounting is concerned with planning, control and decision making. Which of the following relates to planning?**

A Preparation of the annual budget for a cost centre

B Revise the budget for a cost centre

C Compare the actual and expected results for a period

D Implement decisions based on information provided

7 **Monthly variance reports are an example of which one of the following types of management information?**

A Tactical

B Strategic

C Planning

D Operational

8 **Which of the following statements are correct?**

(i) Strategic information is mainly used by senior management in an organisation.

(ii) Productivity measurements are examples of tactical information.

(iii) Operational information is required frequently by its main users.

A (i) and (ii) only

B (i) and (iii) only

C (ii) and (iii) only

D (i), (ii) and (iii)

OBJECTIVE TEST QUESTIONS : SECTION 2

9   Which of the following techniques would be useful for controlling costs?

    (i)   Actual versus flexed budget
    (ii)   Variance analysis
    (iii)   Trend of costs analysis

    A   (i) and (ii) only
    B   (i) and (iii) only
    C   (ii) and (iii) only
    D   (i), (ii) and (iii)

COST IDENTIFICATION AND BEHAVIOUR

10 The following data relate to two output levels of a department:

    Machine hours   18,000   20,000
    Overheads $380,000 $390,000

    The variable overhead rate was $5 per hour.

    The amount of fixed overhead was

    A $230,000
    B $240,000
    C $250,000
    D $290,000

11 Fixed costs are conventionally deemed to be:

    A   Constant per unit of output
    B   Constant in total when production volume changes
    C   Outside the control of management
    D   Those unaffected by inflation

12 Which of the following correctly describes a step cost?

    A   The total cost increases in steps as the level of inflation increases
    B   The cost per unit increases in steps as the level of inflation increases
    C   The cost per unit increases in steps as the level of activity increases
    D   The total cost increases in steps as the level of activity increases

PAPER C01 : FUNDAMENTALS OF MANAGEMENT ACCOUNTING

13 Which of the following pairs are the best examples of semi-variable costs?

- A Rent and rates
- B Labour and materials
- C Electricity and gas
- D Road fund licence and petrol

14 The total cost of direct materials, direct labour and direct expenses is known as:

- A A cost unit
- B A direct cost
- C A prime cost
- D An indirect cost

15 Which of the following are examples of semi-variable costs?

- (i) Raw materials
- (ii) Telephone
- (iii) Electricity
- (iv) Rent

- A (i) and (ii)
- B (ii) and (iii)
- C (i) and (iv)
- D (ii) and (iv)

16 Using the high-low method, the fixed and variable elements of cost for September based on the following information were:

	Units	Cost
July	400	$1,000
August	500	$1,200
September	600	$1,400
October	700	$1,600
November	800	$1,800
December	900	$2,000

- A Fixed cost $200 – Variable cost $200
- B Fixed cost $1,000 – Variable cost $400
- C Fixed cost $200 – Variable cost $1,200
- D Fixed cost $400 – Variable cost $1,000

17 Prime cost is:

    A   The first cost involved in the production process

    B   The material cost of a product

    C   The labour cost of a product

    D   The total of direct costs

18 The information below shows the number of calls made and the monthly telephone bill for the first quarter of last year:

Month	No. of Calls	Cost
January	400	$2,000
February	600	$2,800
March	900	$4,000

Using the high-low method, what was the fixed cost of the line rental each month?

    A $200

    B $300

    C $400

    D $500

19 The following data have been collected for costs D, E, F and G.

Cost	Cost at 300 units activity $	Cost at 550 units activity $
D	2,100	3,850
E	5,340	6,040
F	3,940	3,940
G	360	660

Tick the relevant box below to indicate the behaviour pattern of each cost.

Cost	Variable	Fixed	Semi-variable
D	☐	☐	☐
E	☐	☐	☐
F	☐	☐	☐
G	☐	☐	☐

20 M Ltd manufactures one product. As management accountant at M Ltd you have determined the following information:

		$ per unit
Direct materials		10
Direct labour		29
Direct expenses		3
Production overhead	– variable	7
	– fixed	5
Non-manufacturing costs	– variable	2
	– fixed	4
		60

The prime cost per unit is $_____.

21 **Direct costs are:**

A   costs which can be identified with a cost centre but not identified to a single cost unit

B   costs which can be economically identified with a single cost unit

C   costs which can be identified with a single cost unit, but it is not economic to do so

D   costs incurred as a direct result of a particular decision

22 **The following data relate to two activity levels of an out-patients' department in a hospital:**

| Number of consultations by patients | 4,500 | 5,750 |
| Overheads | $269,750 | $289,125 |

Fixed overheads are $200,000 per period.

The variable cost per consultation is $_____.

23 **Fixed costs are conventionally deemed to be:**

A   constant per unit of output

B   constant in total when production volume changes

C   outside the control of management

D   unaffected by inflation

24

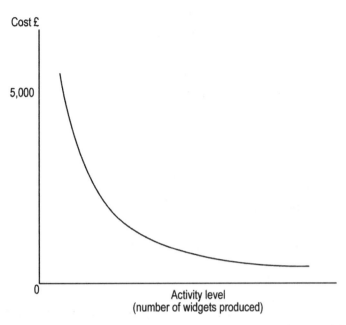

Which of the following descriptions best suits the graph?

A   Total fixed costs

B   Total variable costs

C   Variable costs per unit

D   Fixed costs per unit

25 Variable costs are conventionally deemed to:

A   be constant in total when activity levels alter

B   be constant per unit of activity

C   vary per unit of activity where activity levels alter

D   vary in total when activity levels remain constant

26 Which of the following are direct costs? (tick all that apply)

The depreciation of stores equipment	
The hire of a machine for a specific job	
Royalty paid for each unit of a product produced	
Packaging materials	

PAPER C01 : FUNDAMENTALS OF MANAGEMENT ACCOUNTING

27 **The following details relate to product R:**

Level of activity (units)	1,000	2,000
	$/unit	$/unit
Direct materials	4.00	4.00
Direct labour	3.00	3.00
Production overhead	3.50	2.50
Selling overhead	1.00	0.50
	11.50	10.00

(a) The total fixed cost is $_____.

(b) The variable cost is $_____ per unit.

28 **Which ONE of the following would be classified as direct labour?**

A Personnel manager in a company servicing cars

B Bricklayer in a construction company

C General manager in a DIY shop

D Maintenance manager in a company producing cameras

29 **Overtime premium is:**

A the additional amount paid for hours worked in excess of the basic working week

B the additional amount paid over and above the normal hourly rate for hours worked in excess of the basic working week

C the additional amount paid over and above the overtime rate for hours worked in excess of the basic working week

D the overtime rate

30 When total purchases of raw material exceed 30,000 units in any one period then all units purchased, including the initial 30,000, are invoiced at a lower cost per unit.

Which of the following graphs is consistent with the behaviour of the total materials cost in a period?

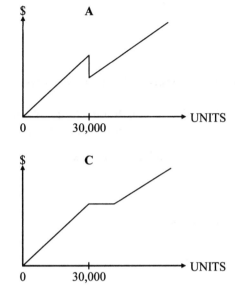
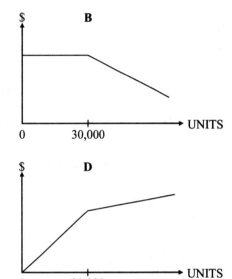

OVERHEAD ANALYSIS

The following data relate to questions 31 and 32

Budgeted machine hours	22,000
Actual machine hours	23,500
Budgeted production overhead	$99,000
Actual production overhead	$111,625

31 The machine hour rate for overhead absorption is

    A $0.22

    B $4.22

    C $4.50

    D $4.75

32 The amount of under/over absorption is

    A $5,875 under-absorbed

    B $5,875 over-absorbed

    C $12,625 under-absorbed

    D $12,625 over-absorbed

33 A method of dealing with overheads involves spreading common costs over cost centres on the basis of benefit received. This is known as

- A Overhead absorption
- B Overhead apportionment
- C Overhead allocation
- D Overhead analysis

34 A vehicle repair company recovers overhead on the basis of chargeable labour hours.

Budgeted overheads for the latest period were $28,800 and actual chargeable labour hours worked were 400. The actual overheads of $26,700 were over-absorbed by $2,280.

The budgeted overhead absorption rate per chargeable labour hour was:

- A $61.05
- B $66.75
- C $72.00
- D $72.45

35 The process of cost apportionment is carried out so that:

- A costs may be controlled
- B cost units gather overheads as they pass through cost centres
- C whole items of cost can be charged to cost centres
- D common costs are shared among cost centres

Questions 36 and 37 are based on the following data

Budgeted labour hours	8,500
Budgeted overheads	$148,750
Actual labour hours	7,928
Actual overheads	$146,200

36 The labour hour overhead absorption rate for the period was:

- A $17.20 per hour
- B $17.50 per hour
- C $18.44 per hour
- D $18.76 per hour

37 Overheads during the period were:

- A Under-absorbed by $2,550
- B Over-absorbed by $2,529
- C Over-absorbed by $2,550
- D Under-absorbed by $7,460

OBJECTIVE TEST QUESTIONS : SECTION 2

38 A company absorbs overheads based on machine hours which are budgeted at 11,250 hours at $23 per hour. If actual machine hours worked were 10,980 hours and overheads were $254,692 then overheads were:

A   Under-absorbed by $2,152

B   Over-absorbed by $4,058

C   Under-absorbed by $4,058

D   Over-absorbed by $2,152

39 Is the following statement true or false?

Overheads will always be under-absorbed when actual overhead expenditure is higher than budgeted for the period.

40 After the initial overhead allocation and apportionment has been completed, the overhead analysis sheet for a factory is as follows.

Overhead cost	Machining	Finishing & packing	Stores	Maintenance
$57,440	$24,100	$17,930	$5,070	$10,340

The costs of maintenance are to be reapportioned to the other three cost centres according to the number of maintenance hours worked, which are as follows.

	Machining	Finishing & packing	Stores	Maintenance
Maintenance hours	3,800	850	50	100

The maintenance cost (to the nearest $) to be apportioned to the machining department is $ _____.

41 A cost centre absorbs production overhead on the basis of machine hours. Last period the overhead was under-absorbed by $20,000. The actual production overhead incurred was $280,000 and 40,000 machine hours were worked.

The overhead absorption rate per machine hour was $ _____.

42 Which of the following can be used as a measure of pre-determined overhead rates in absorption costing?

(i)   Number of units

(ii) Number of labour hours

(iii) Number of machine hours

A   (i) and (ii)

B   (ii) and (iii)

C   (i) and (iii)

D   (i), (ii) and (iii)

43 Which of the following will result in an under absorption of overheads?

A Actual production is above budgeted production

B Actual production is below budgeted production

C Actual overhead is higher than absorbed overhead

D Budgeted overhead is higher than actual overhead

44 The following data relate to two output levels of a department:

Machine hours	17,000	18,500
Overheads	$246,500	$251,750

The variable overhead rate per hour is $3.50. The amount of fixed overheads is:

A $5,250

B $59,500

C $187,000

D $246,500

45 A company absorbs overheads on labour hours which were budgeted at 11,000 with overheads of $55,000. Actual hours worked were 10,900 and actual overheads were $57,500.

Overheads were:

A Under absorbed by $2,500

B Over absorbed by $3,000

C Under absorbed by $3,000

D Over absorbed by $2,500

46 You are given the following information

Budgeted labour hours	48,500
Actual labour hours	49,775
Budgeted overheads	$691,125
Actual overheads	$746,625

The overhead absorption rate (to 2 decimal places) is $_____ per hour.

47 A manufacturing company expects its machinery to be used for 75,000 hours and overheads are absorbed at the rate of $6.40 per machine hour. If actual expenditure totalled $472,560 and 72,600 machine hours were used, which one of the following statements is correct?

A Overhead was under-absorbed by $7,500

B Overhead was under-absorbed by $7,920

C Overhead was over-absorbed by $7,500

D Overhead was over-absorbed by $7,920

OBJECTIVE TEST QUESTIONS : SECTION 2

48   A manufacturing company absorbs overheads based on units produced. In one period 110,000 units were produced and the actual overheads were $500,000. Overheads were $50,000 over-absorbed in the period.

The overhead absorption rate was $_____ per unit.

49   A company has four production departments. Overheads have been apportioned between them as follows:

Department	K	L	M	N
Overheads	$10,000	$5,000	$4,000	$6,000

The time taken in each department to manufacture the company's only product, X, is 5 hours, 5 hours, 4 hours and 3 hours respectively.

If the company recovers overheads on the basis of labour hours and plans to produce 2,000 units, then the overhead absorption rate per unit is $ _____.

50   CRL produces two types of jacket, Blouson and Bomber, in its factory that is divided into two departments, cutting and stitching. The firm wishes to calculate a fixed overhead cost per unit from the following budgeted data.

	Cutting dept	Stitching dept
Direct and allocated fixed overheads	$120,000	$72,000
Labour hours per unit		
Blouson	0.05 hours	0.20 hours
Bomber	0.10 hours	0.25 hours
Budgeted production		
Blouson	6,000 units	6,000 units
Bomber	6,000 units	6,000 units

If fixed overheads are absorbed by reference to labour hours, the fixed overhead cost of a Bomber would be $_____.

51   What is cost apportionment?

A   The charging of discrete identifiable items of cost to cost centres or cost units

B   The collection of costs attributable to cost centres and cost units using the costing methods, principles and techniques prescribed for a particular business entity

C   The process of establishing the costs of cost centres or cost units

D   The division of costs amongst two or more cost centres in proportion to the estimated benefit received, using a proxy e.g. square metres

52   A management consultancy recovers overheads on chargeable consulting hours. Budgeted overheads were $615,000 and actual consulting hours were 32,150. Overheads were under-recovered by $35,000.

If actual overheads were $694,075, the budgeted overhead absorption rate per hour was $_____.

PAPER C01 : FUNDAMENTALS OF MANAGEMENT ACCOUNTING

The following relates to questions 53 and 54

X Ltd has two production departments, Assembly and Finishing, and one service department, Stores.

Stores provides the following service to the production departments:

60% to Assembly and 40% to Finishing.

The budgeted information for the year is as follows:

Budgeted fixed production overheads:

Assembly	$100,000
Finishing	$150,000
Stores	$50,000
Budgeted output	100,000 units

53 The budgeted fixed production overhead absorption rate for the Assembly department will be $_____ per unit.

54 At the end of the year, the total fixed production overheads for the Finishing department were $130,000, and the actual output achieved was 120,000 units.

  (i) The overheads for the Finishing Department were

   under-absorbed ☐
   over-absorbed ☐

  (ii) The amount of the under/over absorption was $_____.

55 P Ltd absorbs overheads on the basis of direct labour hours. The overhead absorption rate for the period has been based on budgeted overheads of $150,000 and 50,000 direct labour hours.

  During the period, overheads of $180,000 were incurred and 60,000 direct labour hours were worked.

  Which of the following statements is correct?

  A Overhead was $30,000 over-absorbed
  B Overhead was $30,000 under-absorbed
  C No under or over-absorption occurred
  D None of the above

56 Budgeted overheads for a period were $340,000. In the event, actual labour hours and overheads were 21,050 hours and $343,825 respectively.

  If there was over-absorption of $14,025, how many labour hours were budgeted?

  A 20,000
  B 20,225
  C 20,816
  D 21,050

OBJECTIVE TEST QUESTIONS : SECTION 2

COST-VOLUME-PROFIT ANALYSIS

57 For the forthcoming year, variable costs are budgeted to be 60% of sales value and fixed costs to be 10% of sales value. If the selling price increases by 10% and fixed costs, variable costs per unit and sales volume remain the same, the effect on contribution would be

- A A decrease of 5%
- B No change
- C An increase of 15%
- D An increase of 25%

58 Product X generates a contribution to sales ratio of 50%. Fixed costs directly attributable to product X are $100,000 per annum.

The sales revenue required to achieve an annual profit of $125,000 is

- A $450,000
- B $400,000
- C $125,000
- D $100,000

59 In order to draw a basic break-even chart, which of the following information would you not require?

- A Selling price
- B Variable cost per unit
- C Fixed cost
- D Margin of safety

60 A company makes a single product which it sells for $10 per unit. Fixed costs are 48,000 and contribution to sales is 40%. If sales were $140,000, what was the margin of safety in units?

- A 2,000
- B 3,000
- C 4,000
- D 5,000

61 Which of the following best describes contribution?

- A Profit
- B Sales value less variable cost of sales
- C Sales value plus variable cost
- D Fixed cost less variable cost

PAPER C01 : FUNDAMENTALS OF MANAGEMENT ACCOUNTING

Questions 62 to 65 are based on the following data

Sales (units)	1,000
Selling price	$10
Variable cost	$6
Fixed costs	$2,500

62 The contribution/sales ratio is:

    A   20%

    B   37.5%

    C   40%

    D   60%

63 The number of units sold in order to break-even is:

    A   100 units

    B   375 units

    C   625 units

    D   1,000 units

64 The margin of safety is:

    A   10%

    B   37.5%

    C   40%

    D   50%

65 How much revenue would we need to generate to produce a profit of $5,000?

    A $10,000

    B $12,250

    C $18,750

    D $23,000

66 If selling price is $100 and unit cost is $40, then:

    A   Gross profit margin is 60% and mark-up is 150%

    B   Gross profit margin is 150% and mark-up is 60%

    C   Gross profit margin and mark-up are the same

    D   Not enough information given to calculate these figures

OBJECTIVE TEST QUESTIONS : SECTION 2

67 Which of the following statements is correct?

A   The point where the total cost line cuts the vertical axis is the breakeven point on a traditional breakeven chart

B   The point where the total cost line cuts the horizontal axis is the breakeven point on a traditional breakeven chart

C   The point where the profit line cuts the horizontal axis is the breakeven point on a profit-volume chart

D   The point where the profit line cuts the vertical axis is the breakeven point on a profit-volume chart

68 Product R sells for $45 per unit and incurs variable cost of $15 per unit and fixed cost of $30,000.

The line drawn on a profit-volume chart will cut the vertical (y) axis at the point where

y = _____

Questions 69 and 70 are based on the following information:

A product has an operating statement for the sales of 1,000 units:

	$
Sales	10,000
Variable Costs	6,000
Fixed Costs	2,500

69 The contribution to sales ratio is:

A   15%

B   25%

C   40%

D   Impossible to determine

70 The margin of safety is:

A   15%

B   25%

C   37.5%

D   40%

PAPER C01 : FUNDAMENTALS OF MANAGEMENT ACCOUNTING

71 H Ltd manufactures and sells one product: J. Total annual sales are planned to be $420,000. Product J has a contribution to sales ratio of 40%. Annual fixed costs are estimated to be $120,000.

The budgeted break-even sales value (to the nearest $1,000) is:

A $200,000

B $300,000

C $105,000

D $120,000

Questions 72 and 73 are based on the following data

A company makes a single product T and budgets to produce and sell 7,200 units each period. Cost and revenue data for the product at this level of activity are as follows.

	$ per unit
Selling price	53
Direct material cost	24
Direct labour cost	8
Other variable cost	3
Fixed cost	7
Profit	11

72 The contribution to sales ratio (P/V ratio) of product T (to the nearest whole number) is _____ %

73 The margin of safety of product T (to the nearest whole number) is _____ % of budgeted sales volume.

DECISION MAKING

RELEVANT COST

74 You are currently employed as a management accountant in an insurance company. You are contemplating starting your own business. In considering whether or not to start your own business, your current salary level would be:

A   a sunk cost

B   an incremental cost

C   an irrelevant cost

D   an opportunity cost

OBJECTIVE TEST QUESTIONS : SECTION 2

75 P Ltd is considering accepting a contract. The materials required for the contract are currently held in stock at a book value of $3,000. The materials are not regularly used by the organisation and currently have a scrap value of $500. Current replacement cost for the materials is $4,500.

The relevant cost to P Ltd of using the materials on this contract is $_____ .

76 In order to complete a special order, a firm needs two materials, S and T. There are ample quantities of both in stock. S is commonly used within the business whereas T is now no longer used for other products.

Information for the two types of material:

	Quantity required for order kg	Original cost $/kg	Replacement cost $/kg	Scrap value $/kg
Material S	2	2.40	4.20	1.80
Material T	3	1.00	1.40	0.40

The relevant cost of materials to be used in completing the order is $_____ .

77 Your company regularly uses material X and currently has in stock 500 kg for which it paid $1,500 two weeks ago.

If this were to be sold as raw material, it could be sold today for $2.00 per kg. You are aware that the material can be bought on the open market for $3.25 per kg, but it must be purchased in quantities of 1,000 kg.

You have been asked to determine the relevant cost of 600 kg of material X to be used in a job for a customer. The relevant cost of the 600 kg is $_____ .

78 The costs most relevant to be used in decision-making are:

A Sunk costs

B Current costs

C Estimated future costs

D Notional and full costs

LIMITING FACTOR ANALYSIS AND MAKE OR BUY DECISIONS

79 Company blue makes a single product which requires $5 of materials, 2 hours of labour and 1 hour of machine time.

There is $500 available for materials each week, 80 hours of labour and 148 hours of machine time. The limiting factor is

A Materials

B Labour

C Machine time

D All of the above

80 A company makes three products as follows:

	A $	B $	C $
Material at $5 per kg	5	2.50	10
Labour at $2 per hour	6	2	2
Fixed costs absorbed	6	2	2
Profit	6	3.50	5
Selling price	23	10	19

Maximum demand is 1,000 each, materials are limited to 4,000 kg, labour is fixed at 1,000 hours. To maximise profits the company should produce

A 1,000 of A

B 1,000 of B

C 1,000 of C

D 333 of each product

81 A company makes and sells three products for which information is as follows.

	Product E $ per unit	Product F $ per unit	Product G $ per unit
Direct labour ($15 per hour)	7.50	22.50	15.00
Direct material ($8 per kg)	12.00	10.00	16.00
Maximum demand per period (units)	380	520	240

Labour hours are limited to 1,300 hours each period and the supply of material is limited to 1,450 kg each period.

What is the company's limiting factor(s)?

A Direct labour

B Direct material

C Both direct material and direct labour

D Neither direct material nor direct labour

82 Simpkins Ltd is currently experiencing a shortage of skilled labour. In the coming quarter only 3,600 hours will be available for the production of the firm's three products for which details are shown below:

Product	X	Y	Z
Selling price per unit	$66	$100	$120
Variable cost per unit	$42	$75	$90
Fixed cost per unit	$30	$34	$40
Skilled labour per unit	0.40 hours	0.50 hours	0.75 hours
Maximum quarterly demand	5,000	5,000	2,000

The optimum production plan that will maximise profit for the quarter is:

A 0 X's 2,200 Y's and 2,000 Z's

B 5,000 X's 200 Y's and 2,000 Z's

C 5,000 X's 3,200 Y's and 0 Z's

D 9,000 X's 0 Y's and 0 Z's

83 Z Ltd manufactures three products, the selling price and cost details of which are given below:

	Product X $	Product Y $	Product Z $
Selling price per unit	75	95	95
Costs per unit:			
Direct materials ($5/kg)	10	5	15
Direct labour ($4/hour)	16	24	20
Variable overhead	8	12	10
Fixed overhead	24	36	30

In a period when direct materials are restricted in supply, the most and the least profitable uses of direct materials are:

	Most profitable	Least profitable
A	X	Z
B	Y	Z
C	X	Y
D	Z	Y

84 WW makes three components – X, Y and Z. The following costs have been recorded:

	X Unit cost $	Y Unit cost $	Z Unit cost $
Variable cost	5.00	16.00	10.00
Fixed cost	4.00	16.60	7.50
Total cost	9.00	32.60	17.50

Another company has offered to supply the components to WW at the following prices:

Component	Price per unit $
X	8.00
Y	14.00
Z	11.00

Which components, if any, should WW consider buying in from the other company?

A   None of the components

B   Component X

C   Component Y

D   Component Z

PAPER C01 : FUNDAMENTALS OF MANAGEMENT ACCOUNTING

85 A company, which manufactures four components (A, B, C and D) using the same machinery, aims to maximise profit. The following information is available:

	Component			
	A	B	C	D
Variable production cost per unit ($)	60	64	70	68
External purchase cost ($)	100	120	130	110
Machine hours per unit to manufacture	4	7	5	6

As it has insufficient machine hours available to manufacture all the components required, the company will need to buy some units of one component from the outside supplier.

Which component should be purchased from the outside supplier?

- A Component A
- B Component B
- C Component C
- D Component D

INVESTMENT APPRAISAL

86 R is due to receive $20,000 in 5 years time. Using a cost of capital of 7.6%, the discount factor will be closest to.

- A 0.059
- B 0.760
- C 0.442
- D 0.693

87 Consider the following statements. Identify if they relate to payback, net present value (NPV) or internal rate of return (IRR). Tick all that apply.

	Payback	NPV	IRR
Should ensure the maximisation of shareholder wealth			
Absolute measure			
Considers the time value of money			
A simple measure of risk			

88 L will receive $25,000 in 6 years time. How much is this worth in today's terms, assuming an interest rate of 5.9%?

Today's value is $_____ . (to the nearest $)

89 Payback considers the whole life of the project.

True or False?

90 (i)   If the IRR is above the company's cost of capital, the project should be accepted

(ii) If NPV is positive, accepting the project would increase shareholder value

(iii) If the payback period is greater than the target period, the project should be accepted.

Which of the above statements are true?

A   (i) and (iii) only

B   (i) and (ii) only

C   (ii) and (iii) only

D   All of them

91 SH Company have decided to expand their manufacturing facility. The cost of this expansion will be $2.7m. Expected cash flows from the expansion are estimated as $750,000 for the first 2 years and $900,000 for the following 2 years.

The IRR of the project is _____% (to 2 decimal places)

92 A project costing $400,000 has the following expected cash flows.

Year	0	1	2	3	4	5
Annual cash flow ($000)	(400)	200	150	100	70	40

The payback period for the project is _____years _____months (to the nearest month)

93 Two NPVs have been calculated for a project at two discount rates:

At discount rate 10%, NPV= $(3,451)

At discount rate 5%, NPV = $387

The IRR for the project is:

A   10.1%

B   5.5%

C   9.5%

D   5.9%

94 A drawback of IRR is that it uses accounting figures rather than cash flows.

True or False?

STANDARD COSTING AND VARIANCE ANALYSIS

95 A standard established for use over a long period of time from which a current standard can be developed is a:

    A   Basic

    B   Ideal

    C   Attainable

    D   Current

Questions 96 and 97 are based on the following information:

In a given week, a factory has an activity level of 120% with the following output:

	Units	Standard minutes each
Product A	5,100	6
Product B	2,520	10
Product C	3,150	12

The budgeted direct labour cost for budgeted output was $2,080.

96 Budgeted standard hours were

    A   1,560

    B   1,872

    C   1,248

    D   1,300

97 Budgeted labour cost per standard hour was

    A $1.33

    B $1.11

    C $1.67

    D $1.60

98 A standard hour is

    A   Always equivalent to a clock hour

    B   An hour with no idle time

    C   The quantity of work achievable at standard performance in an hour

    D   An hour through which the same products are made

OBJECTIVE TEST QUESTIONS : SECTION 2

99 Which of the following statements is incorrect?

- A Both budgets and standards relate to the future
- B Both budgets and standards must be quantified
- C Both budgets and standards are used in planning
- D Both budgets and standards are expressed in unit costs

100 Which type of standard would be most suitable from a motivational point of view?

- A Basic
- B Ideal
- C Attainable
- D Current

Questions 101 to 107 are based on the following budgeted and actual figures for XYZ Ltd in the latest financial year.

Budget

Sales	50,000 units at $100
Production	55,000 units
Materials	110,000 kg at $20 per kg
Labour	82,500 hours at $2 per hour
Variable overhead	82,500 hours at $6 per hour

Actual

Sales	53,000 units at $95
Production	56,000 units
Materials purchased	130,000 kg
Opening inventory of materials	0
Closing inventory of materials	20,000 kg
Materials purchase price	$2,700,000
Labour	85,000 hours paid at $180,000
Labour	83,000 hours worked
Variable overhead	$502,000

101 The sales price variance was

- A $265,000 (A)
- B $265,000 (F)
- C $99,000 (A)
- D $99,000 (F)

45

PAPER C01 : FUNDAMENTALS OF MANAGEMENT ACCOUNTING

102 The sales volume contribution variance was

- A $144,000 (F)
- B $48,000 (F)
- C $300,000 (F)
- D $100,000 (F)

103 The materials usage variance was

- A $20,000 (A)
- B $20,000 (F)
- C $40,000 (A)
- D $40,000 (F)

104 The idle time variance was

- A $2,000 (F)
- B $2,000 (A)
- C $4,000 (F)
- D $4,000 (A)

105 The labour efficiency variance was

- A $4,000 (F)
- B $4,000 (A)
- C $2,000 (F)
- D $2,000 (A)

106 The variable overhead expenditure variance was

- A $2,000 (F)
- B $2,000 (A)
- C $4,000 (F)
- D $4,000 (A)

107 The variable overhead efficiency variance was

- A $6,000 (A)
- B $6,000 (F)
- C $4,000 (A)
- D $4,000 (F)

OBJECTIVE TEST QUESTIONS : SECTION 2

108 A product has standard material cost of $32 (4 kg x $8). During May, 3,000 kg were purchased at a cost of $23,000. The material usage variance for May was $1,600 adverse and the material price variance was $1,000 favourable. What was the actual production level for May?

   A   850 units
   B   750 units
   C   800 units
   D   700 units

Questions 109 and 110 are based on the following information

In week 50 a factory had an activity level of 120%:

	Units	Standard minutes each
Product A	5,100	6
Product B	2,520	10
Product C	3,150	12

The budgeted direct labour cost for budgeted output was $2,080.

109 The budgeted standard hours were:

   A   2,080
   B   1,560
   C   1,300
   D   1,100

110 The budgeted labour cost per standard hour was:

   A $1
   B $1.20
   C $1.60
   D $2

Questions 111 and 112 are based on the following data

PP Ltd has prepared the following standard cost information for one unit of product X:

| Direct materials | 2 kg at $13/per kg | $26.00 |
| Direct labour | 3.3 hours at $4/per hour | $13.20 |

Actual results for the period were recorded as follows:

Production	12,000 units
Materials – 26,400 kg	$336,600
Labour – 40,200 hours	$168,840

All of the materials were purchased and used during the period.

47

PAPER C01 : FUNDAMENTALS OF MANAGEMENT ACCOUNTING

111 The direct material price and usage variances are:

	Material price	Material usage
A	$6,600 (F)	$31,200 (A)
B	$6,600 (F)	$31,200 (F)
C	$31,200 (F)	$6,600 (A)
D	$31,200 (A)	$6,600 (A)

112 The direct labour rate and efficiency variances are:

	Labour rate	Labour efficiency
A	$8,040 (A)	$2,400 (A)
B	$8,040 (A)	$2,400 (F)
C	$8,040 (F)	$2,400 (A)
D	$8,040 (F)	$2,400 (F)

Questions 113 and 114 are based on the following information

The standard selling price of product Y is $34 per unit and the standard variable cost is $20 per unit. Budgeted sales volume is 45,000 units each period.

Last period a total of 46,000 units were sold and the revenue achieved was $1,495,000.

113 The sales price variance for the period was $ _____.

114 The sales volume contribution variance for the period was $ _____.

115 ABC Ltd uses standard costing. It purchases a small component for which the following data are available:

Actual purchase quantity	6,800 units
Standard allowance for actual production	5,440 units
Standard price	$0.85/unit
Purchase price variance (ADVERSE)	($544)

What was the actual purchase price per unit?

A $0.75
B $0.77
C $0.93
D $0.95

116 Trim Ltd's materials price variance for the month of January was $1,000 F and the usage variance was $200 F The standard material usage per unit is 3 kg and the standard material price is $2 per kg. 500 units were produced in the period. Opening stocks of raw materials were 100 kg and closing stocks 300 kg.

Material purchases in the period were:

A   1,200 kg

B   1,400 kg

C   1,600 kg

D   1,800 kg

117 T plc uses a standard costing system, with its material stock account being maintained at standard costs. The following details have been extracted from the standard cost card in respect of direct materials:

8 kg @ $0.80/kg = $6.40 per unit Budgeted production in April 20X9 was 850 units.

The following details relate to actual materials purchased and issued to production during April 20X9 when actual production was 870 units:

Materials purchased   8,200 kg costing $6.888

Materials issued to production   7,150 kg

Which of the following correctly states the material price and usage variances to be reported?

A $286 (A) $152 (A)

B $286 (A) $280 (A)

C $286 (A) $294 (A)

D $328 (A) $152 (A)

118 Z plc uses a standard costing system and has the following labour cost standard in relation to one of its products:

4 hours skilled labour @ $6.00 per hour $24.00

During October 20X9, 3,350 of these products were made which was 150 units less than budgeted. The labour cost incurred was $79,893 and the number of direct labour hours worked was 13,450.

The direct labour variances for the month were:

	Rate	Efficiency
A	$804 (F)	$300 (A)
B	$804 (F)	$300 (F)
C	$807 (F)	$297 (A)
D	$807 (F)	$300 (A)

PAPER C01 : FUNDAMENTALS OF MANAGEMENT ACCOUNTING

Questions 119 –126 are based on the following data

X Ltd operates a standard costing system. The following budgeted and standard cost information is available:

Budgeted production and sales	10,000 units
	$ per unit
Selling price	250
Direct material cost – 3 kg × $10	30
Direct labour cost – 5 hours × $8	40
Variable production overheads – 5 hours × $4	20

Actual results for the period were as follows:

Production and sales	11,500 units
	$
Sales value	2,817,500
Direct material – 36,000 kg	342,000
Direct labour – 52,000 hours	468,000
Variable production overheads	195,000

For all variances, tick the box to indicate whether the variance is adverse or favourable.

119 The direct material price variance is $_____

☐ adverse
☐ favourable

120 The direct material usage variance is $_____

☐ adverse
☐ favourable

121 The direct labour rate variance is $_____

☐ adverse
☐ favourable

122 The direct labour efficiency variance is $_____

☐ adverse
☐ favourable

123 The variable production overhead expenditure variance is $_____

☐ adverse
☐ favourable

OBJECTIVE TEST QUESTIONS : SECTION 2

124 The variable production overhead efficiency variance is $_____

☐ adverse
☐ favourable

125 The sales volume contribution variance is $_____

☐ adverse
☐ favourable

126 The sales price variance is $_____

☐ adverse
☐ favourable

BUDGETING

Questions 127–132 are based on the following data.

Loxo sells office equipment and is preparing his budget for next month.

	Opening inventory Units	Budgeted sales Units	Selling price $ per unit
BAX	63	290	120
DAX	36	120	208
FAX	90	230	51

Closing inventory is 30% of sales units for the month.

All three products are made using Material A, Material B, Labour Grade C and Labour Grade D.

The quantities are as follows:

	Material A Metres	Material B Cubic metres	Labour C Hours	Labour D Hours
BAX	4	2	3	2
DAX	5	3	5	8
FAX	2	1	2	–
Cost	$12 per metre	$7 per cubic metres	$4 per hour	$6 per hour

Loxo's opening inventory of Material A is 142 metres and 81 cubic metres of Material B. He intends to increase this during April, so that there is sufficient raw materials to produce 50 units of each item of equipment.

127 Budgeted sales revenues for the period were

    A $71,440

    B $71,490

    C $72,360

    D $72,490

PAPER C01 : FUNDAMENTALS OF MANAGEMENT ACCOUNTING

128 The budgeted production of FAX's during the month was

    A   203 units

    B   207 units

    C   209 units

    D   219 units

129 The budgeted usage of material A during the month was

    A   2,000 metres

    B   2,144 metres

    C   2,220 metres

    D   2,274 metres

130 The budgeted cost of labour for the month was

    A $16,960

    B $17,368

    C $18,415

    D $19,314

131 Budgeted purchases of material A during the month were:

    A $27,288

    B $32,184

    C $34,162

    D $35,586

132 The budgeted gross profit for the period was

    A $19,200

    B $19,300

    C $19,600

    D $19,700

133 When preparing a production budget the quantity produced equals

    A   Sales + opening inventory + closing inventory

    B   Sales + opening inventory – closing inventory

    C   Sales – opening inventory + closing inventory

    D   Sales – opening inventory – closing inventory

OBJECTIVE TEST QUESTIONS : SECTION 2

134 Which is the last budget to be prepared in the master budget?

- A Sales budget
- B Cash budget
- C Budgeted income statement
- D Budgeted statement of financial position

135 What is budget slack?

- A Additional time built into the planning process to ensure that all budgets are prepared according to the timetable
- B Additional revenue built into the sales budget to motivate the sales team
- C Additional costs built into an expenditure budget to guard against overspending
- D Spare machine capacity that is not budgeted to be utilised

136 A sole trader is preparing a cash budget for January. His credit sales are

Actual	October	$80,000
	November	$60,000
	December	$100,000

Estimated January $50,000.

His recent debt collection experience is

	%
Current month's sales	20
Prior month's sales	60
Sales two months prior	10
Cash discounts taken for payment in the current month	5
Bad debts	5

How much may he expect to collect in January?

- A $70,500
- B $75,500
- C $76,000
- D $80,000

PAPER C01 : FUNDAMENTALS OF MANAGEMENT ACCOUNTING

137 A partnership are preparing their cash budget for September with the following credit sales:

June	$42,460
July	$45,640
August	$47,980
September	$49,480

Recent experience suggests that 60% of customers pay in the month after sale, 25% in month 2, 12% in month 3 with 3% bad debt.

Customers paying in the month after sale are entitled to a 2% discount.

How much cash (to the nearest $) would be collected from credit sales in September?

   A $44,717

   B $45,725

   C $46,372

   D $47,639

Questions 138 – 140 are based on the following budgeted information:

	October	November	December
	Units	Units	Units
Opening inventory	100	120	150
Closing inventory	120	150	130
Sales	500	450	520

The cost of inventory stock is $10 per unit with 40% of purchases for cash, 30% paid in the month after purchase and 30% paid two months after purchase.

138 The budgeted number of units to be purchased in November was

   A   440

   B   480

   C   520

   D   560

139 The value of purchases in October were budgeted to be

   A $4,400

   B $4,800

   C $5,200

   D $5,600

OBJECTIVE TEST QUESTIONS : SECTION 2

140 The amount paid to suppliers in December was budgeted to be

- A $5,000
- B $6,000
- C $7,000
- D $8,000

141 A master budget compromises

- A The budgeted income statement
- B The budgeted cash flow, budgeted income statement and budgeted statement of financial position
- C The budgeted cash flow
- D The capital expenditure budget

142 A company is currently preparing its cash budget for next year. The sales budget is as follows:

	$
March	60,000
April	70,000
May	55,000
June	65,000

40% of its sales are expected to be for cash. Of its credit sales, 70% are expected to pay in the month after sale and take a 2% discount. 27% are expected to pay in the second month after the sale, and the remaining 3% are expected to be bad debts.

The value of sales receipts to be shown in the cash budget for May is

- A $58,491
- B $59,546
- C $60,532
- D $61,475

143 Which of the following costs would not be included in a cash budget.

- A Purchase of non-current asset
- B Wages of administration staff
- C Depreciation of office equipment
- D Direct material purchases

PAPER C01 : FUNDAMENTALS OF MANAGEMENT ACCOUNTING

144 Actual output is 162,500 units

Actual fixed costs (as budgeted) $87,000

Actual expenditure $300,000

Over budget by $18,000 (based on a flexible budget comparison)

The budgeted variable cost per unit is

- A $0.80
- B $1.00
- C $1.20
- D $1.31

145 The budgeted variable cost per unit was $2.75. When output was 18,000 units, total expenditure was $98,000. Fixed overheads were $11,000 over budget, variable costs were the same as budget. The amount budgeted for fixed cost was

- A $30,000
- B $34,250
- C $36,750
- D $37,500

Questions 146 – 148 are based on the following data:

	Budget	Actual
Production	20,000 units	17,600 units
Direct labour	$20,000	$19,540
Variable overhead	$4,200	$3,660
Depreciation	$10,000	$10,000

146 The direct labour variance was

- A $17,600 (A)
- B $19,540 (A)
- C $1,940 (A)
- D $1,940 (F)

147 The variable overhead variance was

- A $3,960 (F)
- B $3,660 (F)
- C $72 (F)
- D $36 (F)

OBJECTIVE TEST QUESTIONS : SECTION 2

148 If volume variance is $5,400F and expenditure variance is $2,400A, the total variance is

    A $3,000F

    B $3,000A

    C $7,800F

    D $7,800A

149 Variable costs are conventionally deemed to

    A   Be constant per unit of output

    B   Vary per unit of output as production volume changes

    C   Be constant in total when production volume changes

    D   Vary in total, from period to period when production is constant

150 Which of the following is a criticism of fixed budgets?

    A   They make no distinction between fixed and variable costs

    B   They provide a formal planning framework that ensures planning does take place

    C   They co-ordinate the various separate aspects of the business by providing a master plan

    D   They provide a framework of reference within which later operating decisions can be taken

151 A company makes 20% of its sales for cash. The following information is available concerning the collection of amounts owing from the credit customers.

Invoices paid in the month after sale	70%
Invoices paid in the second month after sale	27%
Bad debts	3%

Credit customers who pay in the month after sale receive a 2% discount.

Budgeted sales revenues are as follows.

January	February	March
$75,800	$72,900	$66,200

The receipts from customers in March (to the nearest $) are budgeted to be $ _____ .

152
Dougal is preparing a cash budget for July. His credit sales are:

		$
April	(actual)	80,000
May	(actual)	60,000
June	(actual)	40,000
July	(estimated)	50,000

His recent debt collection experience has been as follows:

Current month's sales	20%
Prior month's sales	60%
Sales two months prior	10%
Cash discounts taken	5%
Bad debts	5%

How much may Dougal expect to collect from debtors during July?

A $48,000

B $42,000

C $40,000

D $36,000

153
Macnamara is preparing a cash budget for July. His credit sales are:

		$
April	(actual)	40,000
May	(actual)	30,000
June	(actual)	20,000
July	(estimated)	25,000

His recent debt collection experience has been as follows:

Current month's sales	20%
Prior month's sales	65%
Sales two months prior	10%
Cash discounts taken	2.5%
Bad debts	2.5%

How much may Macnamara expect to collect from debtors during July?

A $19,000

B $20,000

C $21,000

D $24,000

154 The following details have been extracted from the debtor collection records of C Ltd:

Invoices paid in the month after sale	60%
Invoices paid in the second month after sale	25%
Invoices paid in the third month after sale	12%
Bad debts	3%

Invoices are issued on the last day of each month.

Customers paying in the month after sale are entitled to deduct a 2% settlement discount.

Credit sales values for June to September 20X9 are budgeted as follows:

June	July	August	September
$35,000	$40,000	$60,000	$40,000

The amount budgeted to be received from credit sales in September 20X9 is:

A $47,280

B $47,680

C $48,850

D $49,480

155 Which of the following is an NOT an advantage of top-down budgeting:

A It is less time consuming

B It reduces budgetary slack

C It is more likely to motivate managers

D Budgets will be closer to the company's objectives

156 Each unit of product X requires 5 kg of material R. 20% of the input of material R is lost during production. Budgeted output of product X is 1,000 units for the period.

Opening inventory of material R is 200 kg and closing inventory is required to be 100 kg.

What will be the required purchases of material R in the period.

A 6,150 kg

B 6,350 kg

C 4,100 kg

D 3,900 kg

157 A budget which recognises different cost behaviour patterns is designed to change as volume of activity changes is known as:

A A Flexible Budget

B A Flexed Budget

C A Fixed Budget

D None of the above

PAPER C01 : FUNDAMENTALS OF MANAGEMENT ACCOUNTING

Questions 158 – 159 are based on the following data.

	Budget	Actual
Production	10,000 units	9,750 units
Direct labour	$40,000	$40,250
Variable overhead	$50,000	$47,500
Depreciation	$20,000	$20,000

158 The direct labour variance was:

  A $1,250 A

  B $1,250 F

  C $2,500 A

  D $2,500 F

159 The variable overhead variance was:

  A $1,250 A

  B $1,250 F

  C $2,500 A

  D $2,500 F

160 If volume variance is $7,500 adverse, and expenditure is $3,100 favourable, then the total variance is:

  A $4,400 A

  B $7,500 A

  C $3,100 F

  D $4,400 F

161 The following extract is taken from the maintenance cost budget:

Maintenance hours	8,300	8,520
Maintenance cost	$211,600	$216,440

The budget cost allowance for maintenance costs for the latest period, when 8,427 maintenance hours were worked, is $ _____.

INTEGRATED ACCOUNTING SYSTEMS

162 In an integrated cost and financial accounting system, the accounting entries for factory overhead absorbed would be:

- A DR WIP control account
     CR overhead control account

- B DR overhead control account
     CR WIP account

- C DR overhead control account
     CR cost of sales account

- D DR cost of sales account
     CR overhead control accounts

163 The book-keeping entries in a standard cost system when the actual price for raw materials is less than the standard price are:

- A DR raw materials control account
     CR raw materials price variance account

- B DR WIP control account
     CR raw materials control account

- C DR raw materials price variance account
     CR raw materials control account

- D DR WIP control account
     CR raw materials price variance account

164 A company uses standard costing and an integrated accounting system. The accounting entries for an adverse labour efficiency variance are:

- A Debit WIP control account
     Credit labour efficiency variance account

- B Debit labour efficiency variance account
     Credit WIP control account

- C Debit wages control account
     Credit labour efficiency variance account

- D Debit labour efficiency variance account
     Credit wages control account

165 At the end of the period the accounting entries for production overhead over-absorbed would be:

A   DR Overhead control account
    CR Income statement

B   DR Income statement
    CR Overhead control account

C   DR Work in progress account
    CR Overhead control account

D   DR Overhead control account
    CR Work in progress account

166 In an integrated system the accounting entries for the issue of indirect production materials would be:

A   DR Production overhead control account
    CR Work in progress account

B   DR Work in progress account
    CR Production overhead control account

C   DR Production overhead control account
    CR Stores control account

D   DR Stores control account
    CR Production overhead control account

167 In an integrated standard costing system the accounting entries for an adverse labour rate variance would be:

A   DR Labour rate variance account
    CR Work in progress account

B   DR Work in progress account
    CR Labour rate variance account

C   DR Labour rate variance account
    CR Wages control account

D   DR Wages control account
    CR Labour rate variance account

168 When materials are purchased on credit, what would be the relevant cost bookkeeping entry?

A   Debit Work-in progress
    Credit Materials

B   Debit Materials
    Credit Accounts payable

C   Debit Materials
    Credit Work-in-progress

D   Debit Cost of sales
    Credit Materials

169 **Consider the following incomplete data:**

1	Work in progress wages	$30,000
2	Production overhead	$40,000
3	Transfer to finished goods	$350,000
4	Closing inventory	$75,000

What was the value of raw materials brought into production?

A $325,000

B $350,000

C $355,000

D $375,000

170 **In an integrated cost and financial accounting system, the accounting entries for production overhead absorbed would be:**

A DR – WIP control account

   CR – overhead control account

B DR – overhead control account

   CR – WIP account

C DR – overhead control account

   CR – cost of sales account

D DR – cost of sales account

   CR – WIP control account

171 **In the cost ledger the factory cost of finished production for a period was $873,190. The double entry for this is:**

A Dr Cost of sales account

   Cr Finished goods control account

B Dr Finished goods control account

   Cr Work-in-progress control account

C Dr Costing profit and loss account

   Cr Finished goods control account

D Dr Work-in-progress control account

   Cr Finished goods control account

PAPER C01 : FUNDAMENTALS OF MANAGEMENT ACCOUNTING

172 A firm operates an integrated cost and financial accounting system. The accounting entries for absorbed manufacturing overhead would be:

    A   Dr Overhead control account

           Cr Work-in-progress control account

    B   Dr Finished goods control account

           Cr Overhead control account

    C   Dr Overhead control account

           Cr Finished goods control account

    D   Dr Work-in-progress control account

           Cr Overhead control account

COSTING SYSTEMS

JOB AND BATCH COSTING

173 Which of the following are contained in a typical job cost?

    (i)   Actual material cost

    (ii)   Actual manufacturing overheads

    (iii)   Absorbed manufacturing overheads

    (iv)   Actual labour cost

    A   (i), (ii) and (iv)

    B   (i) and (iv)

    C   (i), (iii) and (iv)

    D   (i), (ii), (iii) and (iv)

Questions 174–177 are based on this scenario:

A printing and publishing company has been asked to provide an estimate for the production of 100,000 programmes for the Cup Final 64 pages (32 sheets of paper)

There are four operations in the setup.

1   *Photography* – Each page requires a photographic session costing $150 per session.

2   *Setup costs* – A plate is required for each page. Each plate requires 4 hours of labour at $7 per hour and $35 of materials. Overheads are absorbed at $9.50 per labour hour.

3   *Printing* – Paper costs $12 per 1,000 sheets. Wastage is expected to be 2% of input. Other costs are $7 per 500 programmes and 1,000 programmes are printed per hour of machine time. Overheads are absorbed in printing at $62 per machine hour.

4   *Binding* – These costs are recovered at $43 per hour and 2,500 programmes can be bound in an hour. Profit margin of 10% selling price is needed.

OBJECTIVE TEST QUESTIONS : SECTION 2

174 The printing costs for the job are

- A $44,721
- B $45,632
- C $46,784
- D $47,520

175 The total cost for the job is

- A $64,568
- B $65,692
- C $66,318
- D $67,474

176 The selling price of a programme is

- A $0.70
- B $0.71
- C $0.72
- D $0.75

177 What would be the additional costs charged to the job, if the labour efficiency ratio achieved versus estimate in setup is 90%?

- A $423.80
- B $446.20
- C $469.30
- D $487.10

The following data are to be used for Questions 178 and 179 below:

A firm uses job costing and recovers overheads on direct labour cost.

Three jobs were worked on during a period, the details of which were

	Job 1 $	Job 2 $	Job 3 $
Opening work-in-progress	8,500	0	46,000
Material in period	17,150	29,025	0
Labour for period	12,500	23,000	4,500

The overheads for the period were exactly as budgeted $140,000. Jobs 1 and 2 were the only incomplete jobs.

PAPER C01 : FUNDAMENTALS OF MANAGEMENT ACCOUNTING

178 What was the value of closing work-in-progress?

- A $81,900
- B $90,175
- C $140,675
- D $214,425

179 Job 3 was completed during the period and consisted of 2,400 identical circuit boards. The firm adds 50% to total production costs to arrive at a selling price.

What is the selling price of a circuit board?

- A It cannot be calculated without more information
- B $31.56
- C $41.41
- D $58.33

The following data are to be used for the 180–182:

A firm makes special assemblies to customers' orders and uses job costing. The data for a period are

	Job number AA10 $	Job number BB15 $	Job number CC20 $
Opening WIP	26,800	42,790	0
Material added in period	17,275	0	18,500
Labour for period	14,500	3,500	24,600

The budgeted overheads for the period were $126,000

180 How much overhead should be added to job number CC20 for the period?

- A $24,600
- B $65,157
- C $72,761
- D $126,000

181 Job number BB15 was completed and delivered during the period and the firm wishes to earn 33.3% profit on sales.

What is the selling price of job number BB15?

- A $69,435
- B $75,521
- C $84,963
- D $138,870

OBJECTIVE TEST QUESTIONS : SECTION 2

182 What was the approximate value of closing WIP at the end of the period for job number AA10 and CC20?

   A $58,575
   B $101,675
   C $147,965
   D $217,323

183 A retailer buys in a product for $50 per unit and wishes to achieve 40% gross profit on sales. The selling price is:

   A $70
   B $83.33
   C $90
   D $125

Questions 184 and 185 are based on the following data

A small management consultancy has prepared the following information:

Overhead absorption rate per consulting hour	$12.50
Salary cost per consulting hour (senior)	$20.00
Salary cost per consulting hour (junior)	$15.00

The firm adds 40% to total cost to arrive at a selling price.

Assignment number 652 took 86 hours of a senior consultant's time and 220 hours of a junior consultant's time.

184 What price should be charged for assignment 652?

   A $5,355
   B $7,028
   C $8,845
   D $12,383

185 The total estimated cost of job no. 387 is $2,080. The company requires a profit margin of 20 % of the selling price. The price to be quoted for job no. 387 is $ _____.

186 During a period 3,000 consulting hours were charged out in the ratio of 1 senior to 3 junior hours. Overheads were exactly as budgeted.

   What was the total gross profit for the period?

   A $34,500
   B $48,300
   C $86,250
   D $120,750

PAPER C01 : FUNDAMENTALS OF MANAGEMENT ACCOUNTING

Questions 187 – 189 are based on the information below.

JEDPRINT LTD

Jedprint Ltd specialises in printing advertising leaflets and is in the process of preparing its price list. The most popular requirement is for a folded leaflet made from a single sheet of A4 paper. From past records and budgeted figures, the following data have been estimated for a typical batch of 10,000 leaflets:

Artwork	$65
Machine setting	4 hours @ $22 per hour
Paper	$12.50 per 1,000 sheets
Ink and consumables	$40
Printers' wages	4 hours @ $8 per hour

Note: Printers' wages vary with volume.

General fixed overheads are $15,000 per period during which a total of 600 labour hours are expected to be worked.

The firm wishes to achieve 30% profit on sales.

187 The direct cost of producing 10,000 leaflets was:

- A $350
- B $450
- C $475
- D $525

188 The profit from selling 10,000 units would be:

- A $150
- B $164.16
- C $175.42
- D $192.86

189 The selling price is:

- A $450
- B $525.25
- C $602.26
- D $642.86

PROCESS COSTING

Questions 190–192 are based on the following information:

Input quantity	1,000 kg
Normal loss	10% of input
Process costs	$14,300
Actual output	880 kg Losses are sold for $8 per kg

190 Normal loss is equal to

  A   10 kg

  B   50 kg

  C   100 kg

  D   120 kg

191 The cost per unit is equal to

  A $10

  B $15

  C $20

  D $25

192 The impact on the income statement as a result of the abnormal loss would be

  A $120

  B $130

  C $140

  D $150

Questions 193–198 are based on the following extracts:

Process A

Direct material   2,000 kg at $5 per kg

Direct labour $7,200

Process plant time 140 hours at $60 per hour

Process B

Direct material   1,400 kg at $12 per kg

Direct labour $4,200

Process plant time 80 hours at $72.50 per hour

The department overhead for the period was $6,840 and is absorbed into the costs of each process on direct labour cost. Output from Process A is input into Process B.

	Process A	Process B
Expected output was	80% of input	90% of input
Actual output was	1,400 kg	2,620 kg

There is no finished goods inventory at the beginning of the period and no WIP at either the beginning or the end of the period.

Losses are sold for scrap for 50p per kg from process A and $1.825 per kg from process B.

PAPER C01 : FUNDAMENTALS OF MANAGEMENT ACCOUNTING

193 The departmental overhead absorption rate is what percentage of direct labour costs?

   A   40%

   B   45%

   C   55%

   D   60%

194 The cost per kg of process A is equal to

   A $15.62

   B $16.73

   C $18.58

   D $19.62

195 The cost per kg of process B is equal to

   A $20.50

   B $21.25

   C $21.75

   D $22.25

196 The abnormal loss in process A is

   A   100 kg

   B   200 kg

   C   300 kg

   D   400 kg

197 The abnormal gain in process B is

   A   100 kg

   B   200 kg

   C   300 kg

   D   400 kg

198 The value of the finished goods at the end of process B is

   A $55,235

   B $56,329

   C $56,567

   D $56,985

OBJECTIVE TEST QUESTIONS : SECTION 2

199 The following details relate to the main process of X Ltd, a chemical manufacturer.

Opening WIP

2,000 litres fully completed as to materials and 40% complete as to conversion.

Material input   24,000

Normal loss is 10% of input Output to process 2   19,500 litres

Closing WIP

3,000 litres fully completed as to materials and 45% complete as to conversion.

The numbers of equivalent units to be included in X Ltd's calculation of the cost per equivalent unit, using a weighted average basis of valuation are

	Materials	Conversion
A	21,400	20,850
B	22,500	21,950
C	22,500	20,850
D	23,600	21,950

Questions 200 – 202 are based on the following data

X plc makes one product, which passes through a single process. Details of the process are as follows:

Materials: 5,000 kg at 50p per kg

Labour: $800

Production overheads 200% of labour

Normal losses are 20 per cent of input in the process, and without further processing any losses can be sold as scrap for 30p per kg.

The output for the period was 3,800 kg from the process.

There was no work-in-progress at the beginning or end of the period.

200 What value will be credited to the process account for the scrap value of the normal loss?

    A $300

    B $530

    C $980

    D $1,021

201 What is the value of the abnormal loss?

    A $60

    B $196

    C $230

    D $245

PAPER C01 : FUNDAMENTALS OF MANAGEMENT ACCOUNTING

202 What is the value of the output?

    A $3,724

    B $4,370

    C $4,655

    D $4,900

Questions 203 to 205 are based on the following data

A product is manufactured as a result of two processes, A and B. Details of process B for the month of August were as follows:

Materials transferred from process A	10,000 kg valued at $40,500
Labour costs	1,000 hours @ $5.616 per hour
Overheads	50% of labour costs
Output transferred to finished goods	8,000 kg
Closing work-in-progress	900 kg

Normal loss is 10% of input and losses do not have a scrap value.

Closing work-in-progress is 100% complete for material, and 75% complete for both labour and overheads.

203 What is the value of the abnormal loss (to the nearest $)?

    A   Nil

    B $489

    C $544

    D $546

204 What is the value of the output (to the nearest $)?

    A $39,139

    B $43,488

    C $43,680

    D $43,977

205 What is the value of the closing work-in-progress (to the nearest $)?

    A $4,403

    B $4,698

    C $4,892

    D $4,947

OBJECTIVE TEST QUESTIONS : SECTION 2

Questions 206–207 are based on the following data.

Input	5,000 kg
Normal loss	5%
Process costs	$16,500
Actual output	4,600 kg

Losses are sold for $2.35 per kg.

206 The scrap value of the normal loss was:

- A $587.50
- B $625.50
- C $631.48
- D $700.00

207 The net cost of the abnormal loss was:

- A $100
- B $150
- C $587.50
- D $15,912.50

208 A process produces two joint products A and B. During the month of December, the process costs attributed to complete output amounted to $122,500. Output of X and Y for the period was:

- X   3 tonnes
- Y   4 tonnes

The cost attributed to product X using the weight basis of apportionment was:

- A $45,750
- B $50,150
- C $51,250
- D $52,500

PRESENTING MANAGEMENT INFORMATION

209 Which of the following is not an example of a composite cost unit?

- A Kilowatt hours
- B Meals served
- C Patient days
- D Tonne miles

210 Which of the following would be regarded as a fixed cost of a commercial transport fleet?

- (i) Road fund licence
- (ii) Insurance
- (iii) Diesel
- (iv) Maintenance

A (i) and (ii)
B (i) and (iii)
C (ii) and (iii)
D (ii) and (iv)

211 Which of the following are key differences between the products of service industries and those of manufacturing businesses?

- (i) Intangibility
- (ii) Perishability
- (iii) Heterogeneity
- (iv) Simultaneous production and consumption

A (i) and (ii)
B (i), (ii) and (iii)
C (i), (ii) and (iv)
D (i), (ii), (iii) and (iv)

Questions 212 and 213 are based on the following information:

A company specialises in carrying out tests on animals to see if they have any infection. At present the laboratory carries out 12,000 tests per annum but has the capacity to test a further 6,000 if required.

The current cost of carrying out a trial test is

	$ per test
Materials	115
Technician's fees	30
Variable overhead	12
Fixed overhead	50

To increase capacity to 18,000 it would:

- require a 50% shift premium on technician's fees
- enable a 20% discount to be obtained on materials
- increase fixed costs by $700,000 The current fee per test is $300

OBJECTIVE TEST QUESTIONS : SECTION 2

212   The level of profit based on 12,000 tests is

    A $1,116,000

    B $132,000

    C $1,164,000

    D $1,192,000

213   How much would profit be, if 18,000 tests were carried out?

    A $1,492,000

    B $1,525,000

    C $1,598,000

    D $1,610,000

Questions 214 – 216 are based on the following information:

A transport company has three divisions and you are given the following data.

	Division A	Division B	Division C
Sales ($000)	200	300	250
No. of vehicles	50	20	10
Distance ('000 km)	150	100	50
Identifiable fixed costs	25	30	35

Variable costs are $300,000 for the company as a whole and are estimated to be in the ratio of 1:4:5 respectively for A, B and C.

The fixed costs which are not directly identifiable are $75,000. These are shared equally between the three divisions

214   The contribution of division A was

    A $120,000

    B $145,000

    C $170,000

    D $180,000

215   The contribution per kilometre of division B was

    A $1.25

    B $1.40

    C $1.50

    D $1.80

216   The total net profit of the three divisions was

    A $240,000

    B $285,000

    C $325,000

    D $375,000

PAPER C01 : FUNDAMENTALS OF MANAGEMENT ACCOUNTING

217 Value added can be calculated as follows:

(i) Value added = Sales revenue – Cost of materials and bought-in services

(ii) Value added = Profit + interest + conversion costs

Which of the above statements is/are true?

A (i) only

B (ii) only

C Neither (i) nor (ii)

D (i) and (ii)

218 Calculate the most appropriate unit cost for a distribution company based on the following data:

1	Miles travelled	500,000
2	Tonnes carried	2,500
3	No. of drivers	25
4	Hours worked by drivers	37,500
5	Tonne miles carried	375,000
6	Costs incurred	$500,000

A $1.25

B $1.33

C $1.50

D $1.75

219 For which of the following is a profit centre manager normally responsible?

A Costs only

B Revenues only

C Costs and revenues

D Costs, revenues and investment

220 Reginald is the manager of production department M in a factory which has ten other production departments.

He receives monthly information that compares planned and actual expenditure for department M. After department M, all production goes into other factory departments to be completed prior to being despatched to customers. Decisions involving capital expenditure in department M are not taken by Reginald.

Which of the following describes Reginald's role in department M?

A A cost centre manager

B An investment centre manager

C A profit centre manager

D A revenue centre manager

Section 3

ANSWERS TO PRACTICE QUESTIONS

THE CONTEXT OF MANAGEMENT ACCOUNTING

1   Financial accounting is **externally focused**. It is concerned with the production of statutory accounts for an organisation. These reports are produced as a legal requirement and are published, to be used by parties external to the organisation such as investors, creditors, analysts, government bodies and the public.

   Management accounting is **internally focused**. It is concerned with the provision of information to management to aid decision making. Unlike financial accounting, management accounting is not governed by rules and regulations. It is for internal use only and can be provided in any format. The aim of management accounting is to allow management to make the best decisions in the interest of the organisation in order to drive the business forward in the most successful way.

2   The three main purposes of management accounting are PLANNING, CONTROL and DECISION MAKING.

3   Planning is undertaken at three levels within an organisation: STRATEGIC, MANAGERIAL and OPERATIONAL.

4   The characteristics of good information can be remembered as ACCURATE:

   Accurate
   Complete
   Cost beneficial
   Understandable
   Relevant
   Authoritative
   Timely
   Easy to use

5   The level of detail in information provided at the strategic level tends to be low. Information at this level tends to be highly summarised. Information provided at the operational level tends to be highly detailed.

PAPER C01 : FUNDAMENTALS OF MANAGEMENT ACCOUNTING

6 A shared services centre (SSC) has the following advantages over a dedicated business partner:

- **Cost reduction.** This comes from reduced headcount, premises and associated costs. The SSC, for example, may be located in a geographic area with favourable labour or property rates.

- **Increased quality of service.** The central team can become very experienced and adopt best practice.

- **Consistency** of management information throughout the organisation.

7 The CIMA code of ethics is made up of:

Integrity
Objectivity
Professional competence and due care
Confidentiality
Professional behaviour

8 The disadvantages of business process outsourcing are:

- **Loss of control.** The work is being carried out remotely so management are unable to supervise the function on a day-to-day basis.

- **Over-reliance on external providers.** Often the systems containing the information are not accessible to the organisation, meaning that they are only able to get the information the outsourcers provide. It can also become very difficult to bring the function back in house, as experience and knowledge is lost.

- **Confidentiality risk.** Important information could end up getting into the wrong hands.

- **Loss of quality.** Quality requirements must be specified when the contract is set up and quality control must be put in place to monitor the work of the outsourced function.

9 The purpose of the new designation is to elevate the profession of management accounting around the world. Businesses around the world will recognise the CGMA designation and will be confident that members of CGMA will be able to assist them in making critical business decisions and will contribute to driving strong business performance.

10 Internal environmental costs include:

- Waste disposal costs

- Regulatory costs such as taxes based on levels of emissions

- Decommissioning costs on project completion

COST IDENTIFICATION AND BEHAVIOUR

11 (a) Cost unit – a unit of product or service in relation to which costs are ascertained.

(b) Cost centre – a production or service location, a function, an activity or an item of equipment for which costs are accumulated.

(c) Cost object – anything for which costs can be ascertained, for example a product, service, centre, activity, customer or distribution channel.

12 Costs may be classified as follows:

- By nature – labour, material, expenses
- By purpose – direct, indirect
- By behaviour – fixed, variable, semi-variable

13 A direct cost is a cost which can be clearly identified with the cost object which is being costed. An indirect cost can be attributed to a batch of output, but cannot be directly attributable to a particular cost unit.

A direct cost for a book publisher would be paper. This would be classified as a direct material. An indirect cost could be the factory supervisor's salary. This could be classified as indirect labour.

14 Prime cost is the total of direct costs. This will normally include direct material, direct labour and direct expenses.

15 Match a graph to each of the following costs:

(a) Variable cost per unit – graph 1

(b) Total fixed cost – graph 1

(c) Stepped fixed costs – graph 3

(d) Total variable cost – graph 2

(e) Semi-variable cost – graph 4

16 A semi-variable cost is a cost which contains both fixed and variable components. The fixed part is unchanged by changes in the level of activity, but the variable component will change with the changes in the level of activity.

17 Variable cost per unit = change in cost ÷ change in activity

= (43,000 – 30,000) ÷ (2,800 – 1,500) = **$10 per unit**

Fixed cost = total cost – (variable cost per unit × number of units)

= 43,000 – (10 × 2,800) = **$15,000**

Total cost for 3,000 units = 15,000 + (10 × 3,000) = **$45,000**

18 Marginal cost is the extra cost of making one additional unit.

PAPER C01 : FUNDAMENTALS OF MANAGEMENT ACCOUNTING

19 An overhead cost is expenditure in labour, materials or services which cannot be economically identified with a specific saleable cost unit. Overheads are also referred to as indirect costs.

20 Benefits of cost accounting:

   (i)   Discloses profitable and unprofitable parts of the business
   (ii)   Identifies waste and inefficiency
   (iii) Estimates and fixes selling prices
   (iv)   Values inventories
   (v)   Develops budgets and standards
   (vi)   Analyses changes in profits.

21 (i)   Cost unit
   (ii)   Direct
   (iii) Prime
   (iv)   Overhead or Indirect
   (v)   Centre
   (vi)   Fixed
   (vii) Variable
   (viii) Rent
   (ix)   Raw materials
   (x)   Telephone or Electricity.

22 Fixed and variable costs

   a = Fixed cost
   b = Variable cost

23 High–low method

	Units	Cost
Highest month	900	$2,000
Lowest month	400	$1,000
	500	$1,000

   The additional cost between the highest and lowest month

   $= \dfrac{\$1{,}000}{500 \text{ units}} = \$2$ per unit

   So taking either higher or lower number

   Higher 900 × $2 = $1,800   so fixed cost = $200
   Lower 400 × $2 = $800   so fixed cost = $200

ANSWERS TO PRACTICE QUESTIONS : SECTION 3

24 Total production cost = (3,000 × $2) + $4,000 = $10,000.

25 (i) Axes are drawn where the vertical (y) axis is the total cost and the horizontal (x) axis is the level of activity.

(ii) All recorded data pairs are plotted on the graph as separate points.

(iii) The straight line of best fit is drawn by eye between the plotted points.

(iv) The line of best fit is extrapolated back to cross the y axis. The point where the extrapolated line cuts the vertical axis can be read off as the fixed element of the cost.

(v) The variable element of the cost is established by determining the gradient of the line of best fit.

26 Step cost is a cost which rises in a series of steps, for example, the rent of a second factory.

OVERHEAD ANALYSIS

27 (i) Rent – Floor space

(ii) Power – Megawatt hours

(iii) Depreciation – Capital value

(iv) Cost of canteen facility – No. of workers

(v) Machine maintenance labour – Machine maintenance hours

(vi) Supervision – No. of workers.

28 Rent apportionment

Total occupancy	= 100,000 sq. metres
Annual rent	= $500,000
Cost per sq. metre	= $5
Department A occupancy	= 30,000 sq. metres
Department A rent (30,000 × $5)	= $150,000

29 Methods by which overheads can be absorbed into cost units

(i) Rate per unit

(ii) Percentage of prime cost

(iii) Percentage of direct wages

(iv) Direct labour hour rate

(v) Machine hour rate.

30 (i) Variable overhead absorption rate using high-low method

($356,375 − $338,875) ÷ (16,500 − 14,500) = $8.75 per hour

(ii) At 14,500 labour hours

	$
Total overheads expected	338,875
Variable overheads (14,500 × $8.75)	(126,875)
Estimated total fixed overheads	212,000

31 Total budgeted overheads = $22 per hour

Variable overheads = $8.75 per hour

Therefore fixed overheads = $13.25 per hour

$$\frac{\$212,000}{\$13.25} = 16,000 \text{ labour hours}$$

32 Over/under absorption

	$
Under/over absorption	
Actual overheads	355,050
Absorbed overheads (15,850 × $22)	(348,700)
Under absorption of overheads	6,350

33 (a) overhead absorption – this involves absorbing the overhead into the cost units produced in the production cost centres, using a predetermined overhead absorption rate.

(b) overhead apportionment – this involves spreading common costs over cost centres on the basis of benefit received. For example the cost of rent of the factory buildings may be apportioned on the basis of the floor area used by each department.

(c) overhead allocation – this involves whole items of cost to single cost centres. For example the salary of the production manager can be allocated directly to the production department.

34 Reciprocal servicing occurs when two service cost centres use each other's facilities. For example, if two service cost centres were maintenance and canteen. It is possible that the canteen would use the services of the maintenance department and it is also likely that the staff in the maintenance department would use the canteen. In this example the canteen must pick up a share of the maintenance department cost and at the same time, the maintenance department must pick up a share of the canteen costs.

35 A predetermined overhead absorption rate is calculated by dividing the budgeted costs by the budgeted level of activity.

36 An under- or over-absorption of overheads could occur due to two reasons:

1. The actual level of activity was different from the budgeted level of activity.
2. The actual overhead was different from the budgeted overhead.

37

	Production A	Production B	Service C	Service D
Overhead costs	10,000	25,000	21,000	15,000
Apportion C	9,450	9,450	(21,000)	2,100
Sub total	**19,450**	**34,450**	**0**	**17,100**
Apportion D	5,130	10,260	1,710	(17,100)
Sub total	**24,580**	**47,710**	**1,710**	**0**
Apportion C	770	770	(1,710)	171
Sub total	**25,350**	**48,480**	**0**	**171**
Apportion D	51	103	17	(171)
Sub total	**25,401**	**48,583**	**17**	**0**
Apportion C	8	8	0	1
Apportion D	0	1	0	(1)
TOTAL	**25,409**	**48,592**	**0**	**0**

COST-VOLUME-PROFIT ANALYSIS

38 Contribution — sales value minus variable cost.

39 Break-even volume target

$$\text{Break-even volume target} = \frac{\text{Fixed costs}}{\text{Selling price} - \text{variable cost per unit}}$$

= $1,000 ÷ ($10 − $6) = 250 units

40 Profit targets

$$\text{Volume target} = \frac{\text{Contribution target}}{\text{Unit contribution}}$$

= ($1,000 + $200 + $350) ÷ $4 = 387.5

So rounding up 388 units.

41 Margin of safety

The margin of safety is the difference between budgeted sales volume and break-even sales volume.

Break-even sales = $200,000 ÷ ($10 − $5) = 40,000 units

Budgeted sales = 80,000

So margin of safety = 40,000 or 50% of budgeted sales.

42 (i) Profitability to sales = $\dfrac{\$1{,}500}{\$10{,}000} = 15\%$

    (ii) Contribution to sales = $\dfrac{\$4{,}000}{\$10{,}000} = 40\%$

    (iii) 1   Break-even sales value $\dfrac{\$2{,}500}{40\%} = \$6{,}250$

         2   If selling price is $10 and break-even sales value is $6,250 then unit sales = 625

    (iv) Margin of safety = ($10,000 − $6,250) ÷ $10,000 = 37.5%

If you multiply contribution to sales ratio with margin of safety, you end up with the same figure as the profitability to sales ratio.

43 A break-even chart plots total costs and total revenues at different levels of output. A profit-volume chart shows the net profit or loss at any level of output.

44 For the accountant, both the total cost and sales revenue are shown as straight lines. For the economist, unit cost could rise or fall due to economies or diseconomies of scale and in order to sell more units, the economist would argue that price would need to fall.

DECISION MAKING

RELEVANT COST

45 Relevant costs have the following three features:

    (i) They are FUTURE costs and revenues

    (ii) They are INCREMENTAL.

    (iii) They are CASH FLOWS.

ANSWERS TO PRACTICE QUESTIONS : SECTION 3

46 Examples of non-relevant costs are:

(i) Sunk costs. For example, development costs.

(ii) Committed costs. For example, market research which has been commissioned.

(iii) Non cash flows. For example, depreciation.

(iv) General fixed overheads.

(ii) Net book values.

(iii) Notional costs. For example, notional rent.

47 Opportunity cost represents the best alternative which is forgone in taking the decision. For example if for a project to be undertaken, labour must be withdrawn from making product X, then the contribution lost from being able to sell product X would be an opportunity cost and should be treated as a relevant cost for the project.

LIMITING FACTOR ANALYSIS AND MAKE OR BUY DECISIONS

48 Multiple products

Labour hours (2,000/5) = 400 units of A

Labour hours (2,000/8) = 250 units of B

Materials ($12,000/$20) = 600 units of A

Materials ($12,000/$15) = 800 units of B

Limiting factor is labour.

So

Product A contribution per labour hour $\frac{\$5}{5}$ = $1

Product B contribution per labour hour $\frac{\$6}{8}$ = $0.75

Company maximises its contribution by selling product A, since limiting factor value is higher.

49 A limiting factor is any factor which is in scarce supply and stops the organisation from expanding its activities further.

In such a situation, it then seeks to maximise the contribution per unit of the limiting factor.

50 Contribution per labour hour of X $\dfrac{\$25}{5} = \$5$ (2nd)

Contribution per labour hour of Y $\dfrac{\$40}{6} = \$6.67$ (1st)

Contribution per labour hour of Z $\dfrac{\$32}{8} = \$4$ (3rd)

Quantities produced

	Hours
100 units of Y	600
50 units of X	250
18.75 units of Z	150 (balance)
	1,000

Since it would not be practical to produce 0.75 of a unit, we would produce 18 units of product Z with 6 spare hours.

INVESTMENT APPRAISAL

51 The advantages of the payback method of investment appraisal are:

- It is simple to understand
- It is a simple measure of risk in the project, the longer the payback period, the riskier the project tends to be.
- It uses cash flows rather than accounting profits.

The disadvantages of payback are:

- It is not a measure of absolute profitability
- It ignores the time value of money
- It does not take account of cash flows after the payback period

52 The advantages of the NPV method of investment appraisal are:

- It considers the time value of money
- It is a measure of absolute profitability
- It considers the whole life of the project
- It uses cash flows rather than accounting profits
- It should maximise shareholder wealth

The disadvantages of NPV are:

- It is complex
- It can be hard for non-financial managers to understand
- It requires an estimate of the company's cost of capital

ANSWERS TO PRACTICE QUESTIONS : SECTION 3

53

Year	Cashflow $	Discount factor 10%		Discount factor 20%	
		DF (10%)	PV $	DF (20%)	PV $
0	(190,000)	1	(190,000)	1	(190,000)
1	54,000	0.909	49,086	0.833	44,982
2	68,000	0.826	56,168	0.694	47,192
3	87,000	0.751	65,337	0.579	50,373
4	45,000	0.683	30,735	0.482	21,690
		NPV =	**11,326**	**NPV =**	**(25,763)**

L = 10%

H = 20%

N_L = $11,326

N_H = ($25,763)

IRR = 10 + $\dfrac{11,326}{11,326 - (-25,763)} \times (20 - 10)$

IRR = 13.05%

The IRR is more than the cost of capital, therefore **the project should be accepted.**

54 The time value of money recognises that $1 today is worth more than $1 in a year's time. This is due to the effects of inflation.

In investment appraisal this is dealt with by using discounted cash flow techniques.

STANDARD COSTING AND VARIANCE ANALYSIS

55 Standard costing is a control technique which compares standard costs and revenues with actual results to obtain variances which are used to improve performance.

56 A standard cost is the planned unit cost of the products, components or services produced in a period.

PAPER C01 : FUNDAMENTALS OF MANAGEMENT ACCOUNTING

57 Types of standard

(i) A *basic standard* is a standard established for use over a long period from which a current standard can be developed,

(ii) An *ideal standard* is one which can be attained under the most favourable conditions, with no allowance for normal losses, waste or idle time,

(iii) An *attainable standard* is one which can be attained if a standard unit of work is carried out efficiently. Allowances are made for normal losses,

(iv) A *current standard* is based on current levels of performance. Allowances are made for current levels of loss and idle time, etc.

58 Preparations of standard costs

In general, a standard cost will be subdivided into four key cost elements. They are

(i) Direct materials

(ii) Direct wages

(iii) Variable overhead

(iv) Fixed overhead.

59 A standard hour is the amount of work achievable, at standard efficiency levels in an hour.

60 (i) Budgeted labour costs and standard hours

Actual standard hours produced

Product A $\left(5{,}000 \times \dfrac{5}{60}\right)$ 416.67

Product B $\left(2{,}500 \times \dfrac{10}{60}\right)$ 416.67

Product C $\left(3{,}000 \times \dfrac{15}{60}\right)$ 750.00

                                      1,583.34

Representing 110% of budgeted standard hours

$= 1{,}583.34 \times \dfrac{100}{110}$

= 1,439 budgeted standard hours

(ii) Budgeted labour cost per standard hour

$= \dfrac{\text{Budgeted cost}}{\text{Budgeted standard hours}}$

$= \dfrac{\$5{,}000}{1{,}439}$

= $3.47 per hour

61 Standard cost for cheese and pickle sandwich

	$
2 slices of bread (2 × $0.025)	0.05
50 grams cheese (50/1000 × $3)	0.15
25 grams pickle (25/1000 × $2)	0.05
5 grams butter (5/1000 × $1.50)	0.0075
Cost per sandwich started (95%)	0.2575
Standard material cost (100%)	$ 0.2710

62 Sources of information

Standard materials price may be estimated from:

(i) Quotes/estimates from suppliers

(ii) Industry trends

(iii) Bulk discounts available

(iv) Quality of material

(v) Packaging and carriage inwards charges.

63

	$
5 kgs A at $2	10
3 kgs B at $3	9
4 hours grade X at $5	20
5 hours grade Y at $10	50
Variable overhead (9 × $20)	180
Standard variable cost	269

64 Standards

In setting standards, three things should be remembered.

(i) Their use for control purposes

(ii) Their impact on motivation

(iii) Their relevance to the planning process.

65 A cost variance is a difference between a planned, budgeted or standard cost and the actual cost incurred.

66 Materials variances

An adverse materials price variance and a favourable materials usage variance indicates that there is an inverse relationship between the two. This might be caused by purchasing higher quality material.

67 Variable overhead

It indicates that the work completed took longer than it should have done. It could be caused by employing semi-skilled workers instead of skilled workers who will take longer to complete the job.

68 Labour/overhead efficiency variance

The labour efficiency variance and the variable overhead efficiency variance will total the same number of hours. Their monetary value is likely to be different if their hourly rates are different.

69 (i) Sales price:

480 × ($110 − $100) = $4800 F

(ii) Sales volume contribution:

20 × 50 = $1,000 A

70 (i) Labour rate:

1,000 hours should cost	$4,000
1,000 hours did cost	$4,200
So direct labour rate	$200 A

(ii) Labour efficiency:

700 units should take	1,050 hours
700 units did take	1,000 hours
A saving of	50 hours
So 50 × $4 =	$200 F

71 (i) Material price:

2,250 kg should have cost	$22,500
2,250 kg did cost	$20,500
So material price	$2,000 F

(ii) Material usage:

1,000 units should have used	2,000 kg
1,000 units did use	2,250 kg
So 250 × $10 =	$2,250 A

ANSWERS TO PRACTICE QUESTIONS : SECTION 3

72 (i) The material usage variance, being favourable, indicates that the amount of material used was less than expected for the actual output achieved. This could be caused by the purchase of higher quality materials, which resulted in less wastage than normal.

(ii) The labour rate variance, being favourable, indicates that the hourly wage rate paid was lower than expected. This could be due to employing a lower grade employee than was anticipated in the budget.

(iii) The sales volume contribution variance, being adverse, indicates that the number of units sold was less than budgeted. This may have been caused by the increased sales price of $11 (compared to a budgeted price of $10) which has reduced customer demand, or due to the actions of competitors.

73 Interdependence of variances is the term used to describe the situation when there is a single cause of a number of variances.

For example, the use of a higher grade of labour than was anticipated is likely to cause an adverse labour rate variance, a favourable labour efficiency variance, and possibly a favourable material usage variance (due to more experience of working with materials).

It is important that when variances are reported, the possibility that some of them may have a common cause should be acknowledged, and managers encouraged to work together for the benefit of the organisation.

BUDGETING

74 Aims of budgeting

(i) Planning and co-ordination

(ii) Authorising and delegating

(iii) Evaluating performance

(iv) Discerning trends

(v) To communicate and motivate

(vi) To control.

75 A budget may be defined as a quantitative statement, for a defined period of time which may include planned revenues, expenses, assets, liabilities and cash flows. It provides a focus for the organisation and is part of the strategic process.

76 Items that might be included in a budget manual

(i) An explanation of the budgetary planning and control process

(ii) An organisation chart to show budget responsibilities

(iii) A timetable for budget preparation

(iv) Copies of any forms to be completed by budget holders

(v) The organisation's account codes

(vi) Key assumptions to be made in the planning process

(vii) Name and location of the budget officer

77 Production budget

Required for:

(i) Raw materials

(ii) Direct labour

(iii) Machine hours

(iv) Production overheads

78 Budget centre

A budget centre is a section in an organisation for which control may be exercised and budgets prepared.

79 Budget and forecast

A forecast is a prediction of what is expected to happen, a budget is a quantified, formal plan that the organisation is aiming to achieve.

80 Master budget income statement

	$	$
Sales		450,000
Cost of sales		
Opening inventory	20,000	
Raw materials	120,000	
Direct labour	130,000	
Production overhead	120,000	
	390,000	
Closing inventory	30,000	360,000
Operating margin		90,000
Administration		45,000
Operating profit		45,000

ANSWERS TO PRACTICE QUESTIONS : SECTION 3

81   Types of functional budgets

   (i)   Sales

   (ii)   Production

   (iii) Purchasing

   (iv)   Research and development

   (v)   Human resource management

   (vi)   Logistics.

82   The principal budget factor is the limiting factor since this determines all other budgets.

   In most companies, the level of demand determines the size and scale of the operation which is why many budgetary planning processes begin with the sales budget.

83   A cash budget is a detailed budget of cash inflows and outflows covering both revenue and capital items.

84   Objectives of a cash budget

   The objectives of a cash budget are to anticipate any shortages/surpluses and to provide management information in short- and medium-term cash planning and in planning for longer-term finance for the organisation.

85   Cash collected in March

	$
March sales 10% of 800	80
Feb sales 40% of 600	240
Jan sales 45% of 500	225
	545

86   Purchases in February (units)

Sales	450
Opening inventory	(150)
Closing inventory	120
Purchases in units	420

87 Three months purchases

Purchases in January

	Units
Sales	400
Opening inventory	(100)
Closing inventory	150
	450

Purchases in February (see Question 121) 420 units

Purchases in March

	Units
Sales	420
Opening inventory	(120)
Closing inventory	180
	480

So, 450 + 420 + 480 = 1,350 units

88 Amount paid to suppliers in March

50% of March purchases + 50% of January purchases

= (50% × 480 units × $5) + (50% × 450 units × $5)

= $2,325

89 A flexible budget is a budget which, by recognising different cost behaviour patterns, is designed to change as volume of activity changes.

90 *Advantages*

(i) Fixed budgets make no distinction between fixed and variable costs,

(ii) Fixed budgets take no account of production shortfall.

Disadvantages

(i) Flexible budgets are more expensive to operate.

(ii) In many businesses, especially service industries, most costs are fixed over a budget period.

91 Volume variance

A volume variance is the difference in costs and revenues caused by a difference between the planned level of activity and the actual level of activity.

ANSWERS TO PRACTICE QUESTIONS : SECTION 3

92 Expenditure variance

An expenditure variance is the difference between the budgeted level of expenditure for the actual level of activity and the actual level of expenditure.

93 Flexed budget

An original budget is set at the beginning of the period based on the estimated level of activity. This is, then, flexed to correspond with the actual level of activity.

Consider the following example.

A company manufactures a single product but activity levels vary widely from month to month. The budgeted figures are based on an average activity level of 10,000 units of production each month.

The actual figures for last month are also shown:

	Budget $	Actual $
Direct labour	10,000	9,400
Materials	5,000	4,800
Variable overhead	5,000	4,300
Depreciation	10,000	10,000
Fixed overhead	5,000	5,200
	35,000	33,700
Production	10,000	9,500

	Flexed	Actual	Variance
Production units	9,500	9,500	
	$	$	$
Direct labour	9,500	9,400	100 (F)
Materials	4,750	4,800	50 (A)
Variable overhead	4,750	4,300	450 (F)
Depreciation	10,000	10,000	–
Fixed overhead	5,000	5,200	200 (A)
	34,000	33,700	300 (F)

PAPER C01 : FUNDAMENTALS OF MANAGEMENT ACCOUNTING

INTEGRATED ACCOUNTING SYSTEMS

94 Integrated accounts are a set of accounting records which provide both financial and cost accounts using a common input of data for all accounting purposes.

95 Process 1

Overhead absorbed rate (OAR) $= \dfrac{\text{Budgeted overheads}}{\text{Budgeted level of activity}}$

$= \dfrac{\$125,000}{\$50,000}$ = 250% of direct labour cost

(from work-in-process figures)

Process 2

OAR $= \dfrac{\$105,000}{\$70,000}$ = 150% of direct labour cost

96

Freehold buildings at cost

	$000		$000
Bal b/f	800		

Plant and equipment

	$000		$000
Bal b/f	480		

Provision for depreciation on plant and equipment

	$000		$000
Bal c/f	108		100
		Production overhead control (W1)	8
	108		108
		Bal b/f	108

Raw materials

	$000		$000
Bal b/f	400	Payables	10
Payables	210	Work-in-process 1	136
		Work-in-process 2	44
		Bal c/f	420
	610		610
Bal b/f	420		

Work-in-process 1

	$000		$000
Bal b/f	246	Abnormal loss (W3)	20
Raw materials	136	Work-in-process 2 (W2)	483
Wages	84	Bal c/f	173
Production overhead control (W4)	210		
	676		676
Bal b/f	173		

Work-in-process 2

	$000		$000
Bal b/f	302	Abnormal loss (W6)	33
Raw materials	44	Finished goods (W7)	908
Wages	130	Bal c/f	213
Work-in-process 1 (W2)	483		
Production overhead control (W5)	195		
	1,154		1,154
Bal b/f	213		

Finished goods

	$000		$000
Bal b/f	60	Cost of sales	844
Work-in-process 2 (W7)	908	Bal c/f	124
	968		968
Bal b/f	124		

Receivables

	$000		$000
Bal b/f	1,120	Bank	1,140
Sales	1,100	Bal c/f	1,080
	2,220		2,220
Bal b/f	1,080		

Capital

	$000		$000
		Bal b/f	2,200

Profit retained

	$000		$000
		Bal b/f	220

Payables

	$000		$000
Raw materials	10	Bal b/f	300
Bank	330	Raw materials	210
Bal c/f	170		
	510		510
		Bal b/f	170

Bank

	$000		$000
Receivables	1,140	Bal b/f	464
Bal c/f	466	Wages	200
		Production overhead control	170
		Production overhead control	250
		Payables	330
		Administration overhead	108
		Selling and distribution overhead	84
	1,606		1,606
		Bal b/f	466

Sales

	$000		$000
Bal c/f	2,300	Bal b/f	1,200
		Receivables	1,100
	2,300		2,300
		Bal b/f	2,300

Cost of sales

	$000		$000
Bal b/f	888	Bal c/f	1,732
Finished goods	844		
	1,732		1,732
Bal b/f	1,732		

Abnormal loss

	$000		$000
Bal b/f	9	Bal c/f	62
Work-in-process 1 (W3)	20		
Work-in-process 2 (W6)	33		
	62		62
Bal b/f	62		

Production overhead under/over absorbed

	$000		$000
Production overhead control	23	Bal b/f	21
		Bal c/f	2
	23		23
Bal b/f	2		

Administration overhead

	$000		$000
Bal b/f	120	Bal c/f	228
Bank	108		
	228		228
Bal b/f	228		

Selling and distribution overhead

	$000		$000
Bal b/f	80	Bal c/f	164
Bank	84		
	164		164
Bal b/f	164		

Wages

	$000		$000
Bank	200	Work-in-process 1	84
Bal c/f	14	Work-in-process 2	130
	214		214
		Bal b/f	14

Production overhead control

	$000		$000
Bank	170	Work-in-process 1 (W4)	210
Bank	250	Work-in-process 2 (W5)	195
Depreciation (W1)	8	Under absorption	23
	428		428

Workings

1 Depreciation = 20% × $480,000 × 1/12 = $8,000

2 Transfer from process 1 to process 2 = materials $154,000 + wages $94,000 + overheads $(94,000 × 250%) = $483,000

3 Value of abnormal loss in process 1 = materials $6,000 + wages $4,000 + overheads $(4,000 × 250%) = $20,000

4 Production overhead absorbed in process 1 = $84,000 × 250% = $210,000

5 Production overhead absorbed in process 2 = $130,000 × 150% = $195,000

6 Value of abnormal loss in process 2 = materials $18,000 + wages $6,000 + overheads $(6,000 × 150%) = $33,000

7 Value of transfer from process 2 to finished goods = materials $558,000 + wages $140,000 + overheads $(140,000 × 150%) = $908,000

ANSWERS TO PRACTICE QUESTIONS : SECTION 3

97 The accounting entries for an issue of direct materials to production would be

Debit WIP since this increases the asset

Credit stores control since this decreases the asset materials inventory

98 Control accounts

(i) Stores

(ii) WIP

(iii) Finished goods

(iv) Production overhead

(v) Administration costs

(vi) Marketing costs.

COSTING SYSTEMS

JOB AND BATCH COSTING

99 Job costing is a form of specific order costing in which costs are attributed to individual jobs.

100 Four items which would appear on a job cost sheet are

(i) Materials purchased specifically for the job

(ii) Materials drawn from inventory

(iii) Direct wages

(iv) Direct expenses.

101 Batch costing is a form of specific order costing in which costs are attributed to batches of products.

102 Batch determination

When products are made in batches for inventory, the batch size will be determined by:

(i) The rate of consumption

(ii) Storage costs

(iii) Time required to take down and set up production facilities

(iv) Capacity available in relation to other requirements of the company.

103 Job costing worked example

	Job X	Job Y
	$	$
Direct materials	200	100
Direct wages	500	600
Add: 40% overhead	280	280
Add: 25% of total cost	245	245
Selling price	$1,225	$1,225

Whatever method is chosen for absorbing overhead, there will be an argument to use another method. In job Y, direct wages were higher which would indicate that more workers were used on this job or the same number of workers took longer. So if overhead was based on labour hours, job Y should have been more expensive than job X.

104 Discrepancies between job cost card and financial accounts

(i) Material requisition on job card not recorded

(ii) Direct labour shown as indirect

(iii) Over/under absorption of various overheads.

105 Batch costing worked example

	Produces 10,000	Produces 20,000
	$	$
Artwork	65	65
Machine setting (4 × 22)	88	88
Paper (12.50 × 10) (12.50 × 20)	125	250
Ink and consumables	40	80
Printers wages (4 × 8) (8 × 8)	32	64
	350	547
Fixed overheads absorbed $25 per labour hour	100	200
Total cost	450	747
Profit 30% $\left(\frac{3}{7}\times 450\right)\left(\frac{3}{7}\times 747\right)$	193	320
Selling price	643	1,067
Selling price per 1,000	$64	$53

ANSWERS TO PRACTICE QUESTIONS : SECTION 3

106 Profit for the period

	$
Revenue from 10,000 (64 × $64 × 10)	40,960
Revenue from 20,000 (36 × $53 × 20)	38,160
	79,120
Direct costs 10,000 (64 × $350)	22,400
Direct costs 20,000 (36 × $547)	19,692
	42,092
Fixed overheads	15,000
	57,092

Profit = $79,120 − $57,092 = $22,028

107 Comment on results

(i) Actual hours worked (64 × 4) + (36 × 8) = 544

(ii) Budgeted hours 600

(iii) 56 hours of excess capacity

(iv) Find more 10,000 leaflet jobs to fill capacity since profit per labour hour is higher.

10,000 leaflet job = ($640 × 30%) ÷ 4 = $48

20,000 leaflet job = ($1,060 × 30%) ÷ 8 = $39.75

108 The collective term for job AND batch costing is specific order costing.

The distinguishing features are:

(i) Work is separated as opposed to a continuous flow

(ii) Work can be identified with a particular customer's order

PROCESS COSTING

109 Process costing applies when goods result from a sequence of continuous or repetitive operations or processes. It can be found in brewing, oil refining and food processing.

110 A normal loss is the amount of loss that is expected from the operation of a process. This loss is expected and is based on past experience and is also considered unavoidable.

111 Process and normal loss account

Process account

	Tonnes	$		Tonnes	Price/Tonne	$
Materials	5,000	20,000	Normal loss	500	3	1,500
Labour cost		8,000	Output	4500	7	31,500
Overhead		5,000				
	5,000	33,000		5,000		33,000

$$\text{Cost per tonne of good output} = \frac{\text{total costs} - \text{scrap sales}}{\text{Expected output}} = \frac{33,000 - 1,500}{4,500}$$

$$\$ = 7 / \text{tonne}$$

Normal loss account

	Tonnes	$		Tonnes	$
Process account	500	1,500	Cash/bank	500	1,500

112 Abnormal loss and abnormal gain

The extent to which the actual loss exceeds the normal loss is referred to as the abnormal loss.

An abnormal gain is where the normal loss is less than expected, for example, if material input was 1,000 kgs and normal loss was 10%, if actual output was 950 kgs there would be an abnormal gain of 50 kgs and if actual output was 875 kgs then there would be an abnormal loss of 25 kgs.

113

Process account

	kg	$		kg	$	$
Materials	5,000	25,000	Normal loss	500	2.00	1,000
Process costs		17,490	Output	4,200	9.22	38,724
			Abnormal loss	300	9.22	2,766
	5,000	42,490		5,000		42,490

$$\text{Cost of good output} = \frac{42,490 - 1,000}{4,500} = \$9.22/\text{kg}$$

Net cost is therefore $9.22 - $2.00 = $7.22/kg

300 × $7.22 = $2,166

Abnormal loss account

	kg	$		kg	$
Process a/c	300	2,766	Cash/bank		600
			Income statement		2,166

114

	Units	Percentage completion	Equivalent units
Started and completed	15,000	100%	15,000
Work-in-process	5,000	75%	3,750
			18,750

Cost per equivalent unit = $\dfrac{\$20,625}{18,750}$ = $1.10

Value of completed units = 15,000 × $1.10 = $16,500

Value of WIP = 3,750 × $1.10 = $4,125

115

Process account

	Units	$		Units	$
Input	5,000	14,700	Normal loss	150	150
Direct materials		13,830	Closing WIP (W1)	800	5,160
Direct wages		6,555	Abnormal loss (W1)	120	696
Production overhead		7,470	Output (W1)	3,930	36,549
	5,000	42,555		5,000	42,555

(W1) Equivalent units table

	Total	%	Input EU	%	Material added EU	%	Wages EU	%	Ohd EU
Normal loss	150	0	–	0	–	0	–	0	–
Closing WIP	800	100	800	75	600	50	400	25	200
Abnormal loss	120	100	120	66⅔	80	33⅓	40	16⅔	20
Output	3,930	100	3,930	100	3,930	100	3,930	100	3,930
	5,000		4,850		4,610		4,370		4,150

	$	$	$	$
Costs	14,700	13,830	6,555	7,470
Normal loss scrap value	(150)			
	$14,550	$13,830	$6,555	$7,470
Cost/equivalent unit =	14,550	13,830	6,555	7,470
	4,850	4,610	4,370	4,150
	= $3	= $3	= $1.50	= $1.80

(W1)

Value of output = 3,930 × (3 + 3 + 1.5 + 1.8) = 236,549

Value of WIP = (800 × 3) + (600 × 3) + (400 × 1.5) + (200 × 1.8) = $5,160

Value of abnormal loss = (120 × 3) + (80 × 3) + (40 × 1.5) + (20 × 1.8) = $696

116 Abnormal loss account

	$		$
Process	696	Scrap	120
		Income statement	576
	696		696

117 The abnormal loss could have resulted from the use of poorer quality materials than normal or from inexperienced employees operating the process wrongly.

Abnormal gain could come from higher grade materials and higher grade labour.

PRESENTING MANAGEMENT INFORMATION

118 Service costing is the cost accounting method that can be applied when the business provides a service or a service function within a manufacturing company.

119 Industries using service costing

(i) Road haulage

(ii) Hotels

(iii) Hospitals

ANSWERS TO PRACTICE QUESTIONS : SECTION 3

120 Cost units for service industries

Service	Cost unit
Restaurants	Meals served
Carriers	Tonne-miles
Hospitals	Patient days
Passenger transport	Passenger miles

121 Differences between service and manufacturing industry

(i) **Intangibility:** Output takes the form of performance, for example, a waiter in a restaurant rather than some tangible good,

(ii) **Heterogeneity:** The standard of service industries is variable due to large human input.

(iii) **Simultaneous production and consumption:** Service industries do not have the luxury of storing their product; it is produced and consumed simultaneously,

(iv) **Perishability:** Related to (iii) – if an airline takes off with excess capacity that revenue is then lost forever.

122 Manufacturing and service cost statement

The major differences between a manufacturing and a service cost statement are

(i) In the service sector there is a lack of detailed variance analysis,

(ii) Inventory figures in service industries will be low in relation to turnover,

(iii) Service industries have their own performance measures, for example, hotels occupancy rates.

123 Composite cost unit

A major problem for service industries is to decide a suitable unit to measure the service. Composite cost units take into account a number of factors, for example, in the road haulage industry, tonne miles travelled takes into account not only the distance travelled but also the weight carried.

PAPER C01 : FUNDAMENTALS OF MANAGEMENT ACCOUNTING

Workings for Questions 124 – 127

	Professional services	Vehicles
	$	$
Salaries	40,000	
Car depreciation		6,000
Electricity	1,200	
Fuel		1,800
Insurance		
Office	600	
Vehicles		800
Telephone		
Mobile	1,200	
Office	1,800	
Office rent + rates	8,400	
Postage	500	
Secretarial	8,400	
Vehicle services		1,200
Road tax		280
	62,100	10,080

	Hours
Hours available (2 × 8 × 5 × 45)	3,600
Administration 25%	(900)
Idle time 22.5%	(810)
Chargeable time	1,890
Travel time 25%	472.5
Active time	1,417.5
Effective chargeable hours	
Travel time (472.5 × 1/3)	157.5
+ active time (1,417.5 × 1)	1,417.5
	1,575

124 Hourly rate for client work

$$\frac{\$62,100}{31,575} = \$39.43 \text{ per hour}$$

125 Travel = $\dfrac{\$39.43}{3}$ = $13.14

126 Vehicle rate per mile = $\dfrac{\$10,080}{18,000}$

                           = 56p per mile

127 The method of costing in the last three examples is service costing.

Section 4

ANSWERS TO OBJECTIVE TEST QUESTIONS

THE CONTEXT OF MANAGEMENT ACCOUNTING

1 C

With BPO, the finance function is external to the organisation which can lead to a loss of control.

2 D

The cash flow statement and the income statement would normally be produced by the financial accountant

3

	Management accounting	Financial accounting
Uses historical data		√
Is carried out at the discretion of management	√	
Uses non financial information	√	
Aids planning within the organisation	√	

4 A

(iii) is incorrect as operation level information is usually accurate.

5 C

This is more of an auditing role, which is not one of the main roles of management accounting

6 A

Preparing a budget is concerned with planning. Revising a budget and comparing actual and expected results are part of the control function and implementing decisions is decision making.

PAPER C01 : FUNDAMENTALS OF MANAGEMENT ACCOUNTING

7   A

Remember that tactical information is used to make *short-term* plans, operational is to make *day-to-day* decisions and strategic information is to make *long-term* decisions.

8   D

9   D

All the techniques listed in the question could be used to monitor and control costs.

COST IDENTIFICATION AND BEHAVIOUR

10   D

The calculation is as follows:

Total cost for 18,000 hours	= $380,000
Variable cost = 18,000 × 5	= $90,000
Fixed costs	= $290,000

11   B

The total amount of fixed costs remains unchanged when production volume changes, therefore the unit rate fluctuates.

12   D

Cost behaviour patterns refer to the way that the cost behaves in relation to the level of activity. Therefore options A and B are incorrect. Option C describes a non-linear variable cost.

13   C

The best examples of semi-variable costs are electricity and gas, since there is a cost for the use of the service which is fixed and a further variable cost based on usage.

14   C

On an individual basis, materials, labour and direct expenses are direct costs but collectively, they are often known as prime costs.

15   B

A semi-variable cost such as telephone and electricity is part fixed and part variable. We pay a fixed cost to have access to these services and a variable cost based on usage.

So (ii) and (iii).

ANSWERS TO OBJECTIVE TEST QUESTIONS : SECTION 4

16 C

Highest	900
Lowest	400
Difference	500 units
Difference in cost	$1,000

Variable cost per unit = $2. At 400 units – if variable cost is $2 per unit and total cost is $1,000, then variable cost must be $800, so fixed cost must be $200.

So for September, fixed cost is $200 – so variable cost must be 600 × $2 = $1,200.

17 D

Prime Cost is Direct Materials, Direct Labour and Direct Expenses.

18 C

	Units	Cost
Highest month	900	4,000
Lowest month	400	2,000
	500	2,000

Additional cost = $\dfrac{\$2,000}{500}$ = $4 per unit 500

So taking either higher or lower number:

Higher 900 × $4 = $3,600   Fixed Cost = $400

Lower 4,500 × $4 = $1,600   Fixed Cost = $400

19 D   Variable

  E   Semi-variable

  F   Fixed

  G   Variable

Since cost F is constant for both activity levels it is clearly a fixed cost.

The remaining costs must be divided by the activity level to determine a unit rate at each level.

Costs D and G each result in a constant unit rate at both activity levels. Therefore both are variable costs.

Cost E results in a different unit rate at each activity level. Therefore it must be part fixed and part variable, i.e. it is a semi-variable cost.

20 Prime cost = $(10 + 29 + 3) = $42 per unit.

Prime costs are direct costs, and exclude all overheads.

PAPER C01 : FUNDAMENTALS OF MANAGEMENT ACCOUNTING

21 B

Direct costs are those attributable to a cost unit, which can be economically identified with the unit.

22 The variable cost per consultation is $15.50.

	4,500	5,750
No. of consultations		
Overhead ($)	269,750	289,125
Less: Fixed overhead ($)	(200,000)	(200,000)
Variable cost ($)	69,750	89,125
Variable cost per consultation ($)	15.50	15.50

23 B

This is a straightforward definition question.

24 D

Although total fixed costs are the same at all levels of activity, the fixed cost per unit falls as the activity level increases. The unit cost does not fall in a straight line, but in a curve as shown in the question.

25 B

Variable costs per unit are usually assumed to be constant, regardless of the level of activity within the relevant range. Answer A is incorrect because it describes the behaviour of a fixed cost within the relevant range of activity. Answer C also describes a fixed cost, since the same total fixed cost would be shared over a varying number of units, resulting in a unit cost that varies with changes in activity levels. Answer D is incorrect because total variable costs are conventionally deemed to remain unaltered when activity levels remain constant.

26

The depreciation of stores equipment	
The hire of a machine for a specific job	√
Royalty paid for each unit of a product produced	√
Packaging materials	√

All of these are direct costs because they can be identified with specific cost units. Depreciation is an indirect cost because it cannot be identified with a specific cost unit.

ANSWERS TO OBJECTIVE TEST QUESTIONS : SECTION 4

27 (a) The total fixed cost is $3,000.

(b) The total variable cost is **$8.50 per unit**.

Workings

The direct costs are wholly variable because their cost per unit is the same at both activity levels ($7.00 per unit).

Since we require only one figure for each type of cost in our answer, we can combine the two overhead costs in our workings.

The overhead costs are either wholly fixed or semi-variable because their cost/unit changes. The total overhead costs are:

1,000 units × $4.50 = $4,500

2,000 units × $3.00 = $6,000

Since the total cost also differs it is semi-variable. The high-low method is used:

	Units	$
	2,000	6,000
	1,000	4,500
Difference	1,000	1,500

Variable cost = $1,500/1,000 = $1.50 per unit

Fixed cost = total cost – variable cost

Fixed cost = $6,000 – (2,000 × $1.50) = $3,000

28 B

Managers are not usually classified as direct labour, because their salary cost cannot be traced to specific cost units.

29 B

This is a basic definition of overtime premium.

30 A

The variable cost line become less steep, because the variable cost per unit is less. If extended to zero units of output, the total variable cost line will be $0.

OVERHEAD ANALYSIS

31 C

Machine hour rate = $99,000/22,000 = $4.50 per machine hour

32 A

	$
Overhead absorbed (23,500 hours × $4.50)	105,750
Overhead incurred	111,625
Under-absorbed overhead	(5,875)

33 B

A method of dealing with overheads which involves spreading common costs over cost centres on the basis of benefit received is known as overhead apportionment.

34 D

	$
Actual overheads incurred	26,700
Over absorption	2,280
Overhead absorbed by actual hours	28,980
Overhead rate per hour = $28,980/400	$72.45

35 D

The process of cost apportionment is carried out so that common costs are shared among cost centres.

36 B

$$\frac{\text{Budgeted overheads}}{\text{Budgeted labour hours}} = \frac{£148,750}{8,500}$$

= $17.50 per hour.

37 D

Actual hours × absorption rate

= 7,928 × $17.50 = $138,740

	$
Actual overhead	146,200
Amount absorbed	138,740
Under absorption	7,460

ANSWERS TO OBJECTIVE TEST QUESTIONS : SECTION 4

38 A

Actual overheads	$254,692
Actual hours × absorption rate	
10,980 × $23	$252,540

Overheads were under-absorbed by $2,152.

39 The statement is false.

If the actual activity level is also higher than budgeted then additional overhead will have been absorbed. It is possible for overhead to be over-absorbed in this situation.

40 Maintenance cost per hour in the three cost centres = $10,340/(3,800 + 850 + 50) = $2.20. Cost to be apportioned to machining department = ($2.20 × 3,800 hours) = $8,360

41

	$
Actual overhead incurred	280,000
Under-absorbed overhead	20,000
Overhead absorbed	260,000

Overhead absorption rate per machine hour = $260,000/40,000 = **$6.50**

42 D

Number of units, labour hours and machine hours can all be used as a measure of pre-determined absorption rates. A rate per unit is only valid if every unit of output is identical.

43 B

If actual production is below budgeted production, fixed overheads are spread over fewer units.

44 C

	$
Total Cost of 17,000 hours	246,500
Variable Cost of 17,000 hours (× $3.50)	59,500
Balance Fixed Cost	187,000

45 C

Overhead absorption rate = 55,000/11,000 = $5 per labour hour

Overheads absorbed = 5 × 10,900 =	$54,500
Actual overheads =	$57,500
Under absorption	$3,000

46

The labour hour absorption rate is $14.25 per labour hour.

Absorption rate = Budgeted overheads/budgeted labour hours

= $691,125/48,500 hours

= $14.25 per labour hour.

47 B

	$
Actual overhead expenditure	472,560
Absorbed overheads: 72,600 × $6.40	464,640
Under-absorption of overheads	7,920

48

The overhead absorption rate was $5 per unit.

	$
Actual overheads	500,000
Over-absorbed overhead	50,000
Absorbed overheads	550,000

Units produced: 110,000

Absorption rate = $550,000/110,000 = $5 per unit.

49

The overhead absorption rate per unit is $12.50.

Total overhead = $25,000

Budgeted units = 2,000

Overhead per unit = $25,000/2,000 = $12.50.

Since the company makes only one product, the unit fixed cost can be calculated simply by dividing total overhead by the production volume in units. It is unnecessary to calculate an absorption rate per hour for each department.

ANSWERS TO OBJECTIVE TEST QUESTIONS : SECTION 4

50 The fixed overhead cost of a Bomber would be $20.00.

Cutting department:

Budgeted hours = (6,000 × 0.05) + (6,000 × 0.10) = 900 hours

Absorption rate for the cutting department = $120,000/900 = $133.33.

Stitching department:

Budgeted hours = (6,000 × 0.20) + (6,000 × 0.25) = 2,700 hours

Absorption rate for the cutting department = $72,000/2,700 = $26.67.

Fixed overhead cost of a Bomber = (0.10 × $133.33) + (0.25 × $26.67) = $20.

51 D

This is a simple definition question. Answer A is incorrect because it describes cost allocation. Answers B and C describe cost allocation and absorption as well as cost apportionment.

52 The budgeted overhead absorption rate per hour was $20.50.

	$
Actual overhead	694,075
Under-recovered overhead	35,000
Absorbed overhead	659,075

Actual consulting hours: 32,150

Absorption rate = $659,075/32,150 hours = $20.50 per hour.

53 The budgeted overhead absorption rate for the Assembly Department is $1.30 per unit.

	Assembly $	Finishing $	Stores $
Budgeted overheads	100,000	150,000	50,000
Apportion Stores (60:40)	30,000	20,000	(50,000)
	130,000	170,000	
Budgeted output (units)	100,000	100,000	
Absorption rate per unit	$1.30	$1.70	

54 (i) The overheads for the Finishing Department were over-absorbed.

(ii)

	$
Overhead expenditure incurred	130,000
Overheads absorbed (120,000 units × $1.70)	204,000
Over-absorbed overhead	74,000

55 C

Overhead absorption rate per hour = $150,000/50,000 hours = $3 per hour.

Actual overhead expenditure	180,000
Overheads absorbed (60,000 hours × $3)	180,000
Under- or over-absorption of overhead	Nil

56 A

Overheads actually absorbed = $343,825 + $14,025
= $357,850

∴ Overhead absorption rate = $\dfrac{\$357{,}850}{21{,}050 \text{ hrs}}$ = $17 per hour

∴ Budgeted labour hours = $\dfrac{\$340{,}000}{\$17}$ = 20,000 hours

COST-VOLUME-PROFIT ANALYSIS

57 D

Let us take a numerical example:

	Original	Change	New
Selling price	100	+10%	110
Variable cost	60	–	60
Contribution/unit	40	+10	50

Percentage increase in contribution per unit = 10/40 = 25% increase.

58 A

$\dfrac{\text{Required contribution}}{\text{C/S ratio}}$

= ($100,000 + $125,000) ÷ 0.5 = $450,000

ANSWERS TO OBJECTIVE TEST QUESTIONS : SECTION 4

59 D

The margin of safety can be determined once the chart has been constructed. It is not necessary to know the margin of safety in order to draw the chart.

60 A

Break-even point $= \dfrac{\text{Fixed costs}}{\text{Contribution/sales}}$

$= \dfrac{\$48,000}{0.4} = \$120,000$

If actual sales = $140,000

Margin of safety = $140,000 – $120,000

= $20,000

If selling price = $10 then 2,000 units represents margin of safety.

61 B

The best description of contribution is sales value less variable cost of sales, which is used in marginal costing.

62 C

Contribution ÷ Sales = $4 ÷ $10 = 40%

63 C

Fixed cost ÷ C/S ratio = $2,500 ÷ 0.4 = $6,250

if selling price is $10 then the break-even unit figure is 625 units.

64 B

Margin of safety:

$= \dfrac{\text{Budgeted sales} - \text{Breakeven sales}}{\text{Budgeted sales}}$

= ($10,000 – $6,250) ÷ $10,000 = 0.375

or 37.5%.

65 C

(Profit target + Fixed costs) ÷ C/S ratio = ($5,000 + $2,500) ÷ 0.4 = $18,750

PAPER C01 : FUNDAMENTALS OF MANAGEMENT ACCOUNTING

66 A

Gross profit margin is based on the selling price so, if selling price is $100 and unit cost is $40, the profit is $60 or 60%. Mark-up is based on the unit cost, so a unit cost of $40 which is selling for $100 is a mark-up of 1.5 or 150%.

67 C

The breakeven point on a traditional breakeven chart is where the total cost line and the sales revenue line intersect. This eliminates options A and B.

The breakeven point on a profit-volume chart is where the profit line cuts the horizontal (activity) axis, at zero profit or loss.

68 The profit line will cut the vertical axis at $y = -\$30,000$. This is the loss at zero activity, which is equal to the fixed cost.

69 C

Contribution to Sales Ratio:

Sales	$10,000
Variable Cost	$6,000
Contribution	$4,000

Contribution to sales = $\dfrac{\$4,000}{\$10,000}$ = 40%

70 C

Margin of safety is the difference between budgeted sales volume and break-even sales volume:

Breakeven sales value = Fixed cost ÷ C/S ratio
Breakeven sales value = $2,500 ÷ 0.4 = $6,250
Break-even sales volume = $6,250 ÷ $10 = $625 units

1,000 – 625	=	375
$\dfrac{375}{1,000}$	=	37.5%

71 B

Break-even $\dfrac{\text{Fixed costs}}{\text{C/S ratio}}$ $\dfrac{\$120,000}{0.475}$

= $300,000

ANSWERS TO OBJECTIVE TEST QUESTIONS : SECTION 4

72 The contribution to sales ratio (P/V ratio) of product T is **34%**.

Workings:

Contribution per unit of product T = $(53 – 24 – 8 – 3) = $18

Contribution to sales ratio = 18/53 = 34%

73 The margin of safety of product T is **61%** of budgeted sales volume.

Workings:

Period fixed costs = 7,200 × $7 = $50,400

Breakeven point = $\frac{\$50,400}{\$18}$ = 2,800 units

Margin of safety = (7,200 – 2,800) units = 4,400 units

Margin of safety as percentage of budgeted sales = 4,400/7,200 = 61%

DECISION MAKING

RELEVANT COST

74 **D**

If I started my own business, I would be unable to continue in my current employment. I would therefore have to forgo my current salary. My current salary is therefore an opportunity cost of setting up my own business.

75 The relevant cost of the materials is **$500**.

Since the materials have no alternative use, they will not be replaced. Thus the relevant cost is the scrap proceeds forgone.

76 The relevant cost to be used in completing the order is **$9.60**.

		$
Material S: relevant cost = replacement cost	(2 × $4.20)	8.40
Material T: relevant cost = scrap value	(3 × $0.40)	1.20
		9.60

77 The relevant cost of the 600 kgs is **$1,950**.

The material is in regular use so its resale value is irrelevant. Past values are always irrelevant. If the material is used it must be replaced, but the excess of 400 kgs due to the purchase of 1,000 kgs is not relevant because the material is in regular use.

Thus the relevant cost is: 600 kgs × $3.25 = $1,950

PAPER C01 : FUNDAMENTALS OF MANAGEMENT ACCOUNTING

78 C

Current costs *may* be relevant but only if they are indicative of future costs. Estimated future costs are only relevant if they are cash flows and are expected to occur as a direct consequence of the decision being taken.

LIMITED FACTOR ANALYSIS AND MAKE OR BUY DECISIONS

79 B

Resources available

Materials	= $500
Labour hours	= 80
Machine hours	= 148

Units we could make from materials	100
Labour	40
Machine time	148

Therefore, limiting factor is labour.

80 C

To make 1,000 units of each requires 3,500 kg of material and 5,000 labour hours. Labour is therefore the limiting factor.

To measure contribution we need to add fixed costs absorbed to the profit, so

$$A = \frac{\$12}{3} = \$4$$

$$B = \frac{\$5.50}{1} = \$5.50$$

$$C = \frac{\$7}{1} = \$7$$

Therefore to maximise profits, the company should produce 1,000 units of C.

ANSWERS TO OBJECTIVE TEST QUESTIONS : SECTION 4

81 B

Labour hours required for maximum demand:	Hours
Product E 380 units × 0.5 hr	190
Product F 520 units × 1.5 hr	780
Product G 240 units × 1 hr	240
	1,210

Since 1,300 hours are available, labour is not a limiting factor.

Material required for maximum demand:	Kg
Product E 380 units × 1.5 kg	570
Product F 520 units × 1.25 kg	650
Product G 240 units × 2 kg	480
	1,700

Since only 1,450 kg is available, material supply is a limiting factor.

82 C

Product	X	Y	Z
Contribution per unit	$24	$25	$30
Skilled labour per unit	0.40	0.50	0.75
Contribution per key factor	$60	$50	$40
Rank	1	2	3
Maximum demand	5,000	5,000	2,000
Production	5,000	3,200	
Labour hours	2,000	1,600	

83 B

Product	X	Y	Z
Contribution	41	54	50
Materials	2	1	3
Contribution per LF	$20.50	$54	$16.66
Ranking	2	1	3

PAPER C01 : FUNDAMENTALS OF MANAGEMENT ACCOUNTING

84 C

	X $	Y $	Z $
Variable cost of manufacture	5	16	10
Cost of external purchase	8	14	11
Gain/(loss) from external purchase	(3)	2	(1)

On the assumption that fixed overhead costs would be unaffected by a decision to switch to external purchasing, WW should consider buying only component Y externally.

85 D

Additional cost of buying in (compared with manufacture) per hour:

A	B	C	D
$10	$8	$12	$7

Buy in component with the lowest additional cost per hour (limiting factor).

INVESTMENT APPRAISAL

86 D

Discount factor $= (1 + r)^{-n}$

$= (1 + 0.076)^{-5} = \underline{0.693}$

87

	Payback	NPV	IRR
Should ensure the maximisation of shareholder wealth		√	√
Absolute measure		√	
Considers the time value of money		√	√
A simple measure of risk	√		

88 $25,000 \times (1/(1.059^6))$

or $25,000 × 0.709 = $\underline{\$17,724}$

89 False

Payback considers only up to the point that the initial investment is repaid, it ignores the cash flows after the payback period.

90 B

A project would be accepted under payback of the payback period is less than the company's target period.

91 IRR = 9.25%

Year	Cash flow ($000)	Discount factor (5%)	Present value	Discount factor (%)	Present value
0	(2,700)	1	(2,700)	1	(2,700)
1	750	0.962	721.50	0.909	681.75
2	750	0.907	680.25	0.826	619.50
3	900	0.864	777.60	0.751	675.90
4	900	0.823	740.70	0.683	614.70
		NPV =	220.05	NPV =	(108.15)

L = 5%

H = 10%

N_L = $220.05

N_H = $(108.15)

$$IRR = L + \frac{N_L}{N_L - N_H}(H - L)$$

IRR = 5 + (220.05/(220.05 + 108.15)) × (10 − 5)

= **8.35%**

92 The payback period is 2 years 6 months

Year	0	1	2	3	4	5
Annual cash flow ($000)	(400)	200	150	100	70	40
Cumulative cash flow	(400)	(200)	(50)	50	120	160

Payback is 2 years + (50/100 × 12) months = 2 years 6 months

93 **B**

$$IRR = L + \frac{N_L}{N_L - N_H}(H - L)$$

IRR = 5 + (387/(387 + 3451)) × (10 − 5)

= **5.5%**

94 **False**

IRR uses cash flows.

PAPER C01 : FUNDAMENTALS OF MANAGEMENT ACCOUNTING

STANDARD COSTING AND VARIANCE ANALYSIS

95 A

A standard established for use over a long period of time from which a current standard can be developed is a basic standard.

96 D

Actual standard hours produced

	Hours
Product A $\left(5,000 \times \dfrac{6}{60}\right)$	510
Product B $\left(2,520 \times \dfrac{10}{60}\right)$	420
Product C $\left(3,150 \times \dfrac{12}{60}\right)$	630
	1,560

Budget standard hours = $1,560 \times \dfrac{100}{120} = 1,300$

97 D

Budgeted labour cost per standard hour

$= \dfrac{\text{Budgeted cost}}{\text{Budgeted standard hours}}$

$= \dfrac{\$2,080}{1,300} = \$1.60$

98 C

A standard hour is the quantity of work achievable at standard performance in an hour.

99 D

Standards are expressed in unit costs. Budgets are expressed in aggregate terms.

100 C

An attainable standard is achievable if work is carried out efficiently. An ideal standard can have a negative motivational impact because it makes no allowances for unavoidable losses or idle time, etc. A basic standard is out of date and unrealistic as a basis for monitoring performance. A current standard is based on current levels of performance and so does not provide any incentive for extra effort.

ANSWERS TO OBJECTIVE TEST QUESTIONS : SECTION 4

101 A

Sales price variance

53,000 × $5 = $265,000 (A)

Actual price below budget.

102 A

Standard contribution per unit:

	$ per unit
Sales price	100
Materials (110,000 × $20)/55,000	(40)
Labour (82,500 × $2)/55,000	(3)
Variable overhead (82,500 × $6)/55,000	(9)
Contribution	48

The sales volume contribution variance

3,000 × $48 = $144,000 (F)

103 D

Materials usage variance

Standard usage (56,000 × 2)	112,000 kg
Actual usage	110,000

Used 2,000 kg less than expected at $20 per kg so $40,000 (F).

104 D

Idle time variance is difference between hours paid and hours worked × hourly rate. It is always negative or adverse.

Actual hours paid	85,000
Actual hours worked	83,000

Idle time 2,000 × $2

So $4,000 (A).

105 C

Labour efficiency is the difference between standard time allowed and actual hours.

Standard time (56,000 × 1.5 hours)	84,000 hours
Actual time	83,000 hours
Labour efficiency rate (1,000 × $2)	$2,000 (F)

106 D

Standard rate × actual hours ($6 × 83,000) = $498,000

Actual variable overhead expenditure − $502,000

Variable overhead expenditure variance 4,000 (A)

107 B

Variable overhead efficiency variance

Same hours as labour Question 6.5 1,000 × $6 = $6,000 (F)

108 D

Material purchased	$23,000
Price variance	+ $1,000
Usage variance	− $1,600
Standard price for actual production	$22,400

Actual production = $22,400/32 = **700 units.**

109 C

	hours
Product F – 5,100 × $\frac{6}{60}$	510
Product C – 2,520 × $\frac{10}{60}$	420
Product A – 3,150 × $\frac{12}{60}$	630
	1,560

= 120% of budget, so 1,560/1.2 = 1,300 standard hours

110 C

Budgeted labour cost per standard hour:

$$= \frac{\text{Budgeted cost}}{\text{Budgeted standard hour}} = \frac{£2,080}{1,300}$$

$$= \$1.60$$

ANSWERS TO OBJECTIVE TEST QUESTIONS : SECTION 4

111 A

Materials price variance:

		$
26,400 × $13 =		343,200
Actual		336,600
Favourable		$6,600

Materials usage variance:

		$
Should have used:	12,000 × 2 × $13	= 312,000
Did use	26,400 × $13	= 343,200

$31,200 Adverse.

112 A

Labour rate:

	$
40,200 × $4	160,800
Actual	168,840
Adverse	$8,040

Labour efficiency:

Should have taken:	12,000 × 3.3 × $4	= 158,400
Did take:	40,200 × $4	= 160,800

$2,400 Adverse

113

The sales price variance for the period was **$69,000 adverse**

46,000 units should sell for (× $34)	1,564,000
But did sell for	1,495,000
Sales price variance	69,000 adverse

114

The sales volume contribution variance for the period was **$14,000 favourable**

	Units
Budgeted sales volume	45,000
Actual sales volume	46,000
Sales volume variance in units	1,000 favourable
× standard contribution per unit	$14
Sales volume contribution variance	$14,000 favourable

115 C

Actual purchases at standard price:

6,800 × 85p	$5,780
Adverse price variance	$544
Actual purchases at actual price	$6,324

$$\frac{\$6,324}{\$6,800} = \$0.93$$

116 C

Standard quantity used	500 × 3 = $1,500
Usage variance	100 Favourable
Materials used	1,400
Opening stock	(100)
Closing stock	300
	1,600 kg

117 D

Price variance:

		$
8,200 kg should cost $0.80/kg	=	6,560
Actual cost	=	6,888
		328 (A)

Usage variance:

870 units should use 8 kg each	=	6,960 kg
Actual usage	=	7,150 kg
		190 kg
190 kg @ $0.80/kg	=	$152 (A)

118 D

Rate variance:

		$
Standard cost of actual hours (13,450 × $6)		80,700
Actual cost		79,893
		807 (F)

Efficiency variance:

Standard hours produced (3,350 × 4)		13,400
Actual hours		13,450
Extra hours		50 (A)

Variance = 50 × $6 = $300 (A)

119 The direct material price variance is *$18,000 favourable*.

Workings:

	$
36,000 kg should cost (× $10)	360,000
but did cost	342,000
Variance	18,000 F

120 The direct material usage variance is $15,000 adverse.

Workings:

11,500 units should use (× 3 kg)	34,500 kg
but did use	36,000 kg
Difference	1,500 kg
× std price per kg	× $10
Variance	$15,000 A

121 The direct labour rate variance is $52,000 adverse.

Workings:

	$
52,000 hours should cost (× $8)	416,000
but did cost	468,000
Variance	52,000 A

122 The direct labour efficiency variance is $44,000 favourable.

Workings:

11,500 units should take (× 5 hours)	57,500 hours
but did take	52,000 hours
Difference	5,500 hours
× std rate per hour	× $8
Variance	$44,000 F

123 The variable production overhead expenditure variance is $13,000 favourable.

Workings:

	$
52,000 hours should have cost (× $4)	208,000
but did cost	195,000
Variance	13,000 F

124 The variable production overhead efficiency variance is $22,000 favourable.

Workings:

Variance in hours from labour efficiency variance	= 5,500 hours
× standard variable production overhead per hour	× $4
Variance	$22,000 F

ANSWERS TO OBJECTIVE TEST QUESTIONS : SECTION 4

125 The sales volume contribution variance is $240,000 favourable.

Workings:

Actual sales volume	11,500 units
Budget sales volume	10,000 units
Variance in units	1,500 favourable
× standard contribution per unit $(250 – 30 – 40 – 20)	× $160
Sales volume contribution variance	$240,000 favourable

126 The sales price variance is $57,500 adverse.

Workings:

	$
11,500 units should sell for (× $250)	2,875,000
But did sell for	2,817,500
Sales price variance	57,500 adverse

BUDGETING

127 B

Budgeted sales

BAX (290 × $120)	$34,800
DAX (120 × $208)	$24,960
FAX (230 × $51)	$11,730
	$71,490

128 C

	FAX
	Units
Sales	230
Closing inventory	69 (30%)
	299
Opening inventory	90 (given)
Production	209

133

129 D

Material used is based on production

	Metres
BAX (314 × 4)	1,256
DAX (120 × 5)	600
FAX (209 × 2)	418
	2,274

130 B

Labour C		Labour D	
	Hours		Hours
(314 × 3)	942	(314 × 2)	628
(120 × 5)	600	(120 × 8)	960
(209 × 2)	418		–
	1,960		1,588

So, (1,960 × $4) + (1,588 × $6)

= $7,840 + $9,528

= $17,368

131 B

	Metres
Materials used	2,274
See Question 115 for workings of the materials used figure	
Closing inventory 50 × (4 + 5 + 2)	
Enough to produce 50 units of each	550
	2,824
Opening inventory (given)	(142)
	2,682

Therefore, 2,682 × $12 = $32,184.

ANSWERS TO OBJECTIVE TEST QUESTIONS : SECTION 4

132 D

Unit cost

	BAX	DAX	FAX
	$	$	$
Material A	48	60	24
Material B	14	21	7
Labour C	12	20	8
Labour D	12	48	–
	86	149	39

	$
BAX (290 × $(120 – 86))	9,860
DAX (120 × $(208 – 149))	7,080
FAX (230 × $(51 – 39))	2,760
	19,700

133 C

Production budget

Sales – opening inventory + closing inventory.

134 D

The last budget to be prepared in the master budget is the budgeted statement of financial position.

135 C

Budget slack is the intentional overestimating of costs or underestimating of revenues to ensure that the budget is achievable.

136 B

Cash in January

	$
Jan sales (20% × 95% × $50,000)	9,500
Dec sales (60% × $100,000)	60,000
Nov sales (10% × $60,000)	6,000
	75,500

135

PAPER C01 : FUNDAMENTALS OF MANAGEMENT ACCOUNTING

137 A

Cash collected in September

	$
August ($47,980 × 98% × 60%)	28,212.24
July ($45,640 × 25%)	11,410.00
June ($42,460 × 12%)	5,095.20
	44,717.24

138 B

Purchases in November

	Units
Sales	450
Opening inventory	(120)
Closing inventory	150
	480

139 C

Purchases in October

	Units
Sales	500
Opening inventory	(100)
Closing inventory	120
Purchases	520

So, 520 × $10 = $5,200.

140 A

Payment to suppliers (December)

	$
December purchases (40% × 500 × $10)	2,000
November purchases (30% × 480 × $10)	1,440
October purchases (30% × 520 × $10)	1,560
	5,000

141 B

A master budget comprises the budgeted cash flow, budgeted income statement and budgeted statement of financial position.

ANSWERS TO OBJECTIVE TEST QUESTIONS : SECTION 4

142 C

Cash received in May

	$
May sales (40% × $55,000)	22,000
April sales (60% × 70% × 98% × $70,000)	28,812
March sales (60% × 27% × $60,000)	9,720
	60,532

143 C

Depreciation is a non cash item and should be excluded from the cash budget.

144 C

Budgeted expenditure	$282,000
Less: Fixed costs	$87,000
Total variable costs	$195,000

Variable cost per unit = $\dfrac{195,000}{162,500}$ = $1.20

145 D

	$
Actual expenditure	98,000
Less: Fixed cost over budget	11,000
Standard expenditure for 18,000 units	87,000
Less: Variable cost (18,000 × $2.75)	49,500
Budgeted fixed cost	37,500

146 C

Standard cost of direct labour	$1 per unit
17,600 units should have cost	$17,600
17,600 units did cost	$19,540
Direct labour variance is	$1,940 (A)

147 D

Variable overhead should have cost	$3,696
$\left(\dfrac{£4,200}{20,000} \times 17,600\right)$	
Actual variable overhead	$3,660
Variable overhead variance	$36 (F)

148 A

$
5,400 (F)
2,400 (A)
_____
3,000 (F)

149 A

Variable costs are conventionally deemed to be constant per unit of output.

150 A

A criticism of fixed budgets is that they make no distinction between fixed and variable costs.

151

The receipts from customers in March (to the nearest $) are budgeted to be $69,620

	$
20% received in cash = 20% × $66,200	13,240.00
Credit sales from February (80% × 70% × 98% × $72,900)	40,007.52
Credit sales from January (80% × 27% × $75,800)	16,372.80
Total receipts from customers	69,620.32

152 C

50,000 × 20%	$10,000
40,000 × 60%	$24,000
60,000 × 10%	$6,000
	$40,000

ANSWERS TO OBJECTIVE TEST QUESTIONS : SECTION 4

153 C

25,000 × 20%	$5,000
20,000 × 65%	$13,000
30,000 × 10%	$3,000
	$21,000

154 D

60% of August sales less 2% discount:

60,000 × 60% × 98%	$35,280
25% July sales	
$40,000 × 25%	$10,000
12% of June sales	
$35,000 × 12%	$4,200
	$49,480

155 C

Bottom –up budgets involve more participation from managers, therefore they are more likely to motivate managers.

156 A

Material required for 1,000 units = 1,000 × 5 kg = 5,000 kg.

Input required = 5,000 ÷ 0.8 = 6,250 kg

Purchases required = 6,250 – 200 + 100 = 6,150 kg

157 A

A flexible budget is a budget which by recognising different cost behaviour patterns is designed to change as volume of activity changes.

158 A

Standard cost of direct labour	$4 per unit
9,750 units should have cost	$39,000
9,750 units did cost	$40,250
Direct labour is	$1,250 A

159 B

Variable overhead should be	$5 per unit
Actual production × standard overhead – 9,750 × $5	$48,750
Actual variable overhead	$47,500
	$1,250 F

160 A

Volume	$7,500 A
Expenditure	$3,100 F
	$4,400 A

161

The budget cost allowance for maintenance costs for the latest period, when 8,427 maintenance hours were worked, is $214,394

Hours	$
8,520	216,440
8,300	211,600
220	4,840

Variable maintenance cost per hour = $4,840/220 = $22

Fixed maintenance cost = $216,440 – (8,520 hours × $22) = $29,000

Budget cost allowance for 8,427 hours = $29,000 + (8,427 × $22) = $214,394

INTEGRATED ACCOUNTING SYSTEMS

162 A

In an integrated cost and financial accounting system, the accounting entries for factory overhead absorbed would be

DR WIP control account

CR overhead control account.

163 A

The book-keeping entries in a standard cost system when the actual price for raw materials is less than the standard price are

DR Raw materials control account

CR Raw materials price variance account.

ANSWERS TO OBJECTIVE TEST QUESTIONS : SECTION 4

164 B

A company which found that they had an adverse labour efficiency variance should

Debit labour efficiency variance account

Credit WIP control account.

165 A

Over-absorbed overhead is transferred from the overhead control account as a credit in the income statement.

166 C

Indirect production costs, such as the cost of indirect materials, are collected in the debit side of the production overhead control account pending their later absorption into work in progress.

167 C

An adverse variance is debited in the relevant variance account. This eliminates options B and D. The variance arose at the point of payment of the wages therefore the credit entry is made in the wages control account.

168 B

Debit Materials

Credit Accounts Payable

169 C

WIP Control Account:

Wages	$30,000	Finished goods	$350,000
Production	$40,000	Closing inventory	$75,000
Raw materials	$355,000		
	$425,000		$425,000

The raw materials is the balancing figure of $355,000.

170 A

Production overhead is collected in the overhead control account during the period. From there it is absorbed as a debit in the work in progress account, using a predetermined overhead absorption rate.

DR WIP control account

CR overhead control account.

171 B

DR Finished Goods Control Account

CR Work-in-Progress Account

172 D

In a cost accounting system, the absorption of manufacturing overhead represents a cost to be charged for work-in-progress with the corresponding bookkeeping entry being a credit to the overhead control account.

COSTING SYSTEMS

JOB AND BATCH COSTING

173 C

Overhead cost is absorbed into job costs using a pre-determined absorption rate. It is not usually possible to identify the actual manufacturing overhead costs related to specific jobs.

174 C

	$
Paper *	39,184
Other costs $\left(\dfrac{100{,}000 \times 7}{500}\right)$	1,400
Machine hours (100 × $62)	6,200
	46,784

*Paper = [(100,000 × 32) ÷1,000] × ($12 ÷ 0.98)

175 A

Total costs

			$
1	Photography (64 × $150)		9,600
	Set up	$	
	Labour (64 × 4 × $7)	1,792	
	Materials (64 × $35)	2,240	
	Overhead (256 × $9.50)	2,432	
			6,464
3	Printing (as per Question 8.2)		46,784
4	Binding (40 × $43)		1,720
			64,568

ANSWERS TO OBJECTIVE TEST QUESTIONS : SECTION 4

176 C

Selling price = ($64,568 ÷ 0.9) = $71,742 ÷ 100,000 = $0.72

177 C

Estimated setup hours = 256

$$\frac{256}{0.9} = 284.4 \text{ hours}$$

Additional costs (284.4 – 256) × $16.50 = $469.30

178 D

	Job 1	Job 2	Total
	$	$	$
Opening WIP	8,500	–	8,500
Materials	17,150	29,025	46,175
Labour	12,500	23,000	35,500
Overheads	43,750	80,500	124,250
	81,900	132,525	214,425

Total labour for period = $(12,500 + 23,000 + 4,500) = $40,000

Overhead absorption rate = $\frac{\$140,000}{\$40,000}$ = 350% of labour cost

179 C

	Job 3
	$
Opening WIP	46,000
Labour	4,500
Overheads (3.5 × $4,500)	15,750
Total production costs	66,250
Profit 50%	33,125
Selling price of 2,400	99,375
Selling price per unit	$41.41

180 C

Overhead absorption

$$\frac{24,600}{24,600 + 14,500 + 3,500} \times \$126,000 = \$72,761$$

PAPER C01 : FUNDAMENTALS OF MANAGEMENT ACCOUNTING

181 C

	$
WIP	42,790
Materials	–
Labour	3,500
Overhead	10,352
	56,642

Overhead = [3,500 ÷ (24,600 + 14,500 + 3,500)] × $126,000 = $10,352

Sales price = $\dfrac{\$56{,}642}{66\,\frac{2}{3}} \times 100 = \$84{,}963$

182 D

	AA10 $	CC20 $	Total $
Opening WIP	26,800		
Materials	17,275	18,500	
Labour	14,500	24,600	
Overhead	42,887	72,761	
Total	101,462	115,861	217,323

183 B

$50/(1–0.4) = $83.33

184 D

Senior	86 hours at $20	$1,720
Junior	220 hours at $15	$3,300
Overheads	306 hours at $12.50	$3,825
Total cost		$8,845
Mark-up	(40%)	$3,538
Selling price		**$12,383**

185

The price to be quoted for job no. 387 is $2,600

The profit is expressed as a percentage of the selling price.

Therefore selling price = $2,080/0.8 = $2,600

ANSWERS TO OBJECTIVE TEST QUESTIONS : SECTION 4

186 A

Senior	750 hours at $20	$15,000
Junior	2,250 hours at $15	$33,750
Overheads	3,000 hours at $12.50	$37,500
Total cost		$86,250
Mark-up	**(40%)**	**$34,500**

187 A

Direct cost of producing 10,000 leaflets:

	$
Artwork	65
Machine setting	88
Paper	125
Ink	40
Wages	32
	350

188 D

Profit from selling 10,000 units:

Direct Cost	350
Overheads	100
Total Cost	450

Profit = $\frac{30}{70} \times 450 = 192.86$

189 D

Selling Price = Total Cost	450
× Profit	192.86
	642.86

PROCESS COSTING

190 C

Normal loss is equal to 10% of 1,000 kg = 100 kgs

145

PAPER C01 : FUNDAMENTALS OF MANAGEMENT ACCOUNTING

191 B

The cost per unit	$
Process costs	14,300
Less: Normal loss scrap	800
	13,500

Cost per unit = $\frac{\$13,500}{900}$ = $15

192 C

	$
Abnormal loss cost (20 × $15)	300
Less: Scrap value (20 × $8)	160
	140

193 D

Departmental overhead absorption rate = $6,840 ÷ ($7,200 + $4,200)

= 60% of direct labour cost

194 C

Process A

Cost/kg = $\frac{\text{Total cost} - \text{scrap value of normal loss}}{\text{Expected output}}$

Total costs

	$
Direct materials (2,000 kg × $5)	10,000
Direct labour	7,200
Process plant time (140 hours × $60)	8,400
Departmental overhead	4,320
	29,920
Less: Scrap value of normal loss	
(20% × 2,000 × $0.50)	200
	29,720
	$29,720

Cost per kg = $\frac{\$29,720}{1,600 \text{ kg}}$

= $18.575/kg

ANSWERS TO OBJECTIVE TEST QUESTIONS : SECTION 4

195 C

Process B

	$
Process A (1,400 kg × $18.575)	26,005
Direct labour	4,200
Direct materials (1,400 kg × $12)	16,800
Process plant time (80 × $72.50)	5,800
Departmental overhead	2,520
	55,325
Less: Scrap value of normal loss (2,800 kg × 10% × $1.825)	511
	54,814
	$54,814

$$\text{Cost per kg} = \frac{\$54,814}{2,520}$$

$$= \$21.75/\text{kg}$$

196 B

Process A

	kg		kg
Input	2,000	Process B	1,400
		Normal loss	400
		Abnormal loss	200
	2,000		2,000

197 A

Process B

	kg		kg
Input from process A	1,400	Normal loss	280
Direct materials	1,400	Finished goods	2,620
Abnormal gain	100		
	2,900		2,900

Abnormal gain = 100 kg

198 D

Value of finished goods = 2,620 × $21.75

= $56,985

199 D

Process account

	litres		litres
Opening WIP	2,000	Normal loss	2,400
Input	24,000	Output	19,500
		Closing WIP	3,000
		Abnormal loss	1,100
	26,000		26,000

Equivalent units table

	Materials		Conversion	
	%	EU	%	EU
Output	100	19,500	100	19,500
Abnormal loss	100	1,100	100	1,100
Closing WIP	100	3,000	45	1,350
		23,600		21,950

200 A

Normal loss = 20% × 5,000 kg = 1,000 kg

Value = 1,000 kg × 30p = $300.

201 C

Abnormal loss = 1,200 − 1,000 = 200 kg

$$\text{Cost per unit} = \frac{\text{Process costs} - \text{normal loss scrap value}}{\text{Input} - \text{normal loss}}$$

= [($5,000 × 0.5) + $800 + (200% × $800) − $300] ÷ (5,000 − 1,000)

= $\frac{\$4,600}{4,000}$ = $1.15 × 200 kg = $230

202 B

Value = 3,800 kg × $1.15 = $4,370.

ANSWERS TO OBJECTIVE TEST QUESTIONS : SECTION 4

203 D

Flow of units

Input = Output + Closing WIP + Normal loss + Abnormal loss

10,000 = 8,000 + 900 + 10% (10,000) + 100 (bal)

	Output	Abnormal loss	Closing WIP	Total
	\multicolumn{4}{c}{**Equivalent units**}
Materials	8,000	100	900 (100%)	9,000
Labour and overheads	8,000	100	675 (75%)	8,775

Costs per EU:

Materials $\dfrac{\$40,500}{9,000} = \$4.50$

Labour and overheads ($5,616 × 1.5) ÷ 8,775 = $0.96

Abnormal loss value = 100 × $5.46 = $546.

204 C

Output value = 8,000 × $5.46 = $43,680.

205 B

Closing WIP value:

	$
900 × $4.50	4,050
675 × $0.96	648
	4,698

206 A

Normal loss = 250 kg

Scrap value = 250 × $2.35 = $587.50.

207 B

Expected Output	2,750 kg
Actual Output	2,600 kg
Volume of abnormal loss	150 kg

Cost per unit $3.35 − Scrap value of normal loss $2.35,

So 150 × $1.00 = $150.00.

208 D

Cost attributed to Product X:

3 × $122,500 = $52,500

149

PAPER C01 : FUNDAMENTALS OF MANAGEMENT ACCOUNTING

PRESENTING MANAGEMENT INFORMATION

209 B

The odd one out is meals served since this only takes into account one factor.

210 A

Road fund licence and insurance costs are costs which are not based on activity.

Diesel and maintenance would be classified as variable costs. Maintenance costs at the very least are semi-variable costs.

211 D

Intangibility, perishability, heterogeneity and simultaneous production and consumption are all features of service industry and are therefore different from manufacturing industry.

212 A

12,000 capacity

	$000	$000
Fees (12,000 × $300)		3,600
Variable costs		
Materials (12,000 × $115)	1,380	
Wages (12,000 × $30)	360	
Variable overhead (12,000 × $12)	144	
		1,884
Contribution		1,716
Fixed overhead (12,000 × $50)		600
Profit		1,116

213 C

18,000 tests

	$000	$000
Fees (18,000 × $300)		5,400
Variable costs		
Materials (18,000 × $115 × 80%)	1,656	
Wages (360 + (6 × 30 × 150%))	630	
Variable overhead (144 × 150%)	216	
		2,502
Contribution		2,898
Fixed overhead		1,300
		1,598

Workings for Questions 214 – 216

	Division A	Division B	Division C
	$000	$000	$000
Sales	200	300	250
Variable costs	30	120	150
Contribution	170	180	100
Identifiable fixed costs	25	30	35
Other fixed costs	25	25	25
Profit	120	125	40

214 C

Division A = Sales – variable cost

= $200,000 – $30,000 = $170,000

215 D

Division B

Total contribution $180,000

Distance travelled   100,000 km

Contribution per km = $1.80

216 B

Total net profit = $120,000 + $125,000 + $40,000 = $285,000.

PAPER C01 : FUNDAMENTALS OF MANAGEMENT ACCOUNTING

217 B

Characteristics of Service Costing:

(i) High levels of indirect costs as a proportion of total costs, e.g. rent for a restaurant.   YES

(ii) Use of composite cost units, e.g. tonne mile.   YES

(iii) Use of equivalent units. This is used in process costing.   NO

So B – (i) and (ii).

218 B

The most appropriate cost unit in this example is the tonne mile:

$$\frac{£500{,}000}{375{,}000} = \$1.33$$

219 C

Answer A relates to a cost centre, answer B to a revenue centre and answer D to an investment centre.

220 A

He is only responsible for costs.

Section 5

MOCK ASSESSMENT 1

1. **Which ONE of the following would be classified as direct labour?**

    A   Personnel manager in a company servicing cars

    B   Cleaner in a cleaning company

    C   General manager in a DIY shop

    D   Maintenance manager in a company producing cameras

2. **The principal budget factor is the**

    A   factor which limits the activities of the organisation and is often the starting point in budget preparation

    B   budgeted revenue expected in a forthcoming period

    C   main budget into which all subsidiary budgets are consolidated

    D   overestimation of revenue budgets and underestimation of cost budgets, which operates as a safety factor against risk

3. **Management accounting is mainly used by company shareholders.**

    True or false?

4. X Ltd operates an integrated cost accounting system. The Work-in-Progress Account at the end of the period showed the following information:

    Work-in-Progress Account

	$		$
Stores ledger a/c	100,000	?	200,000
Wage control a/c	75,000		
Factory overhead a/c	50,000	Balance c/d	25,000
	225,000		225,000

    The $200,000 credit entry represents the value of the transfer to the:

    A   Cost of sales account

    B   Material control account

    C   Sales account

    D   Finished goods inventory account

5 X Ltd absorbs overheads on the basis of machine hours. Details of budgeted and actual figures are as follows:

	Budget	Actual
Overheads	$1,250,000	$1,005,000
Machine hours	250,000 hours	220,000 hours

(a) Overheads for the period were:

under-absorbed ☐

over-absorbed ☐

(b) The value of the under/over absorption for the period was $ _____

6 In an integrated bookkeeping system, when the actual production overheads exceed the absorbed production overheads, the accounting entries to close off the production overhead account at the end of the period would be:

	Debit	Credit	No entry in this account
Production overhead account			
Work in progress account			
Income statement			

7 ST are considering making an investment of $1.2m on launching a new product. They have undertaken some market research and have estimated that the new product could generate the following cash flows:

Year 1: $240,000

Year 2: $265,000

Year 3: $240,000

Year 4: $660,000

Year 5: $290,000

Calculate the payback period for the project and decide which of the following statements is true if ST require payback within 4 years.

A Payback period is 4 years 4 months, therefore project should be undertaken

B Payback period is 4 years 4 months, therefore project should not be undertaken

C Payback period is 3 years 8 months, therefore project should be undertaken

D Payback period is 3 years 8 months, therefore project should not be undertaken

8   **A Limited has completed the initial allocation and apportionment of its overhead costs to cost centres as follows.**

Cost centre	Initial allocation
	$000
Machining	190
Finishing	175
Stores	30
Maintenance	25
	420

The stores and maintenance costs must now be reapportioned taking account of the service they provide to each other as follows.

	Machining	Finishing	Stores	Maintenance
Stores to be apportioned	60%	30%	–	10%
Maintenance to be apportioned	75%	20%	5%	

After the apportionment of the service department costs, the total overhead cost of the production departments will be (to the nearest $000):

Machining $ _____

Finishing $ _____

9   **The budgeted contribution for R Limited last month was $32,000. The following variances were reported.**

Variance	$
Sales volume contribution	800 adverse
Material price	880 adverse
Material usage	822 favourable
Labour efficiency	129 favourable
Variable overhead efficiency	89 favourable

No other variances were reported for the month.

The actual contribution earned by R Limited last month was

A $31,440

B $32,960

C $31,360

D $32,560

PAPER C01 : FUNDAMENTALS OF MANAGEMENT ACCOUNTING

10 The following scattergraph has been prepared for the costs incurred by an organisation that delivers hot meals to the elderly in their homes.

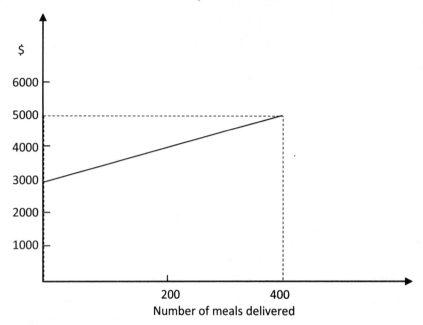

Based on the scattergraph:

	Total fixed cost	Variable cost per unit
A	$5,000	$5.00
B	$3,000	$5.00
C	$3,000	$10.00
D	$3,000	$10.00

11 Which of the following statements are true?

(1) Information used by strategic management tends to be summarised.

(2) Information used by strategic management tends to be historical

(3) Information used by operational management tends to be subjective

(4) Information used by operational management tends to be provided frequently

A (1), (2) and (4) only

B (1), (3) and (4) only

C (2) and (3) only

D (1) and (4) only

12 A project requires an initial investment of $450,000. The following cash flows have been estimated for the life of the project:

Year	1	2	3	4
Cash flow ($000)	120,000	150,000	160,000	120,000

The company uses NPV to appraise projects. Using a discount rate of 7%, the NPV of the project is $_____.

Questions 13 and 14 are based on the following data

X Ltd has two production departments, Assembly and Finishing, and one service department, Stores.

Stores provide the following service to the production departments: 60% to Assembly and 40% to Finishing.

The budgeted information for the year is as follows:

Budgeted production overheads:

Assembly	$100,000
Finishing	$150,000
Stores	$50,000
Budgeted output	100,000 units

13 The budgeted production overhead absorption rate for the Assembly Department will be $_____ per unit.

14 At the end of the year, the total of all of the production overheads debited to the Finishing Department Production Overhead Control Account was $130,000, and the actual output achieved was 100,000 units.

    (a) The overheads for the Finishing Department were:

        under-absorbed _____

        over-absorbed _____

    (b) The value of the under/over absorption was $

15 R Ltd has been asked to quote for a job. The company aims to make a profit margin of 20% on sales. The estimated total variable production cost for the job is $125.

Fixed production overheads for the company are budgeted to be $250,000 and are recovered on the basis of labour hours. There are 12,500 budgeted labour hours and this job is expected to take 3 labour hours.

Other costs in relation to selling, distribution and administration are recovered at the rate of $15 per job.

The company quote for the job should be:

    A $175

    B $240

    C $200

    D $250

PAPER C01 : FUNDAMENTALS OF MANAGEMENT ACCOUNTING

16   Which of the following would NOT be included in a cash budget? Tick all that would NOT be included.

☐ Depreciation

☐ Provisions for doubtful debts

☐ Wages and salaries

The following information is required for Questions 17 and 18

X Ltd is preparing its budgets for the forthcoming year.

The estimated sales for the first four months of the forthcoming year are as follows:

Month 1   6,000 units
Month 2   7,000 units
Month 3   5,500 units
Month 4   6,000 units

40% of each month's sales units are to be produced in the month of sale and the balance is to be produced in the previous month.

50% of the direct materials required for each month's production will be purchased in the previous month and the balance in the month of production.

The direct material cost is budgeted to be $5 per unit.

17   The production budget for Month 1 will be C _____ units.

18   The material cost budget for Month 2 will be $ _____.

19   When calculating the material purchases budget, the quantity to be purchased equals

   A   material usage + materials closing inventory – materials opening inventory

   B   material usage – materials closing inventory + materials opening inventory

   C   material usage – materials closing inventory – materials opening inventory

   D   material usage + materials closing inventory + materials opening inventory

20   The following extract is taken from the overhead budget of X Ltd:

Budgeted activity	50%	75%
Budgeted overhead	$100,000	$112,500

The overhead budget for an activity level of 80% would be:

   A $160,000

   B $115,000

   C $120,000

   D $150,000

21 Which of the following would be included in the cash budget, but would not be included in the budgeted income statement? Tick all that are correct.

Repayment of a bank loan.

Proceeds from the sale of a non-current asset.

Bad debts write off.

22

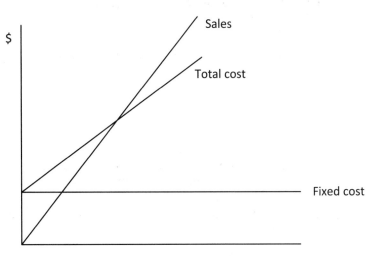

This graph is known as a

A   semi-variable cost chart

B   conventional breakeven chart

C   contribution breakeven chart

D   profit volume chart

23 The following details have been extracted from the payables records of X Limited:

Invoices paid in the month of purchase	25%
Invoices paid in the first month after purchase	70%
Invoices paid in the second month after purchase	5%

Purchases for July to September are budgeted as follows:

July	$250,000
August	$300,000
September	$280,000

For suppliers paid in the month of purchase, a settlement discount of 5% is received. The amount budgeted to be paid to suppliers in September is $ _____

24

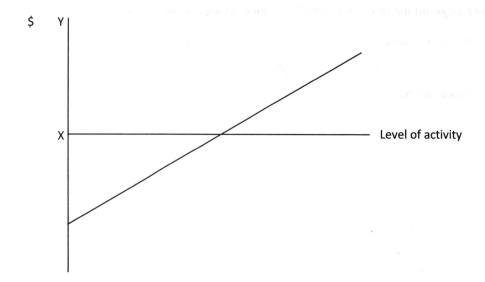

The difference in the values ($) between point X and point Y on the profit volume chart shown above represents:

A   contribution

B   profit

C   breakeven

D   loss

25

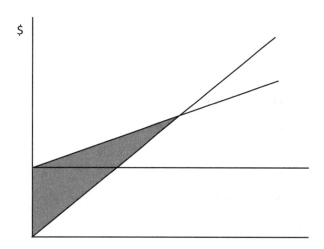

The shaded area on the breakeven chart shown above represents:

A   loss

B   fixed cost

C   variable cost

D   profit

26   In a standard cost bookkeeping system, when the actual material usage has been greater than the standard material usage, the entries to record this in the accounts are:

	Debit	Credit	No entry in this account
Material usage variance account			
Raw material control account			
Work-in-progress account			

27   R Ltd makes one product, which passes through a single process. Details of the process for period 1 were as follows:

	$
Material cost – 20,000 kg	26,000
Labour cost	12,000
Production overhead cost	5,700
Output	18,800 kg
Normal losses	5% of input

There was no work-in-progress at the beginning or end of the period. Process losses have no value.

The cost of the abnormal loss (to the nearest $) is $_____.

28   The labour requirement for a special contract are 250 skilled labour hours (paid $10 per hour) and 750 semi-skilled labour hours (paid $8 per hour).

At present skilled labour is in short supply, and all such labour used on this contract will be at the expense of other work which generates $12 contribution per hour (after charging labour costs). There is currently a surplus of 1,200 semi-skilled labour hours, but the firm temporarily has a policy of no redundancies.

The relevant cost of labour for the special contract is:

A $3,000

B $8,500

C $9,000

D $5,500

29   For decision-making purposes, which of the following are relevant costs?

(i)   Avoidable cost

(ii)   Future cost

(iii)   Opportunity cost

(iv)   Sunk costs

PAPER C01 : FUNDAMENTALS OF MANAGEMENT ACCOUNTING

30 Which of the following would be produced by a management accountant?

    A   Budget

    B   Cash flow statement

    C   Income statement

    D   Statement of financial position

Questions 31 and 32 are based on the following data

PP Ltd has prepared the following standard cost information for one unit of product X:

Direct materials	2 kg at $13/per kg	$26.00
Direct labour	3.3 hours at $4/per hour	$13.20

Actual results for the period were recorded as follows:

Production	12,000 units
Materials – 26,400 kg	$336,600
Labour – 40,200 hours	$168,840

All of the materials were purchased and used during the period.

31 The direct material price and usage variances are:

	Material price	Material usage
A	$6,600 (F)	$31,200 (A)
B	$6,600 (F)	$31,200 (F)
C	$31,200 (F)	$6,600 (A)
D	$31,200 (A)	$6,600 (A)

32 The direct labour rate and efficiency variances are:

	Labour rate	Labour efficiency
A	$8,040 (A)	$2,400 (A)
B	$8,040 (A)	$2,400 (F)
C	$8,040 (F)	$2,400 (A)
D	$8,040 (F)	$2,400 (F)

Questions 33 and 34 are based on the following information

The standard selling price of product Y is $34 per unit and the standard variable cost is $20 per unit. Budgeted sales volume is 45,000 units each period.

Last period a total of 46,000 units were sold and the revenue achieved was $1,495,000.

33 The sales price variance for the period was $ _____.

34 The sales volume contribution variance for the period was $ _____.

35 Which of the following are characteristics of service costing?

　　(i)　High levels of indirect costs as a proportion of total costs

　　(ii)　Use of composite cost units

　　(iii)　Use of equivalent units

　　A　(i) only

　　B　(i) and (ii) only

　　C　(ii) only

　　D　(ii) and (iii) only

36 A company requires 600 kg of raw material Z for a contract it is evaluating. It has 400 kg of material Z in inventory that was purchased last month. Since then the purchase price of material Z has risen by 8% to $27 per kg. Raw material Z is used regularly by the company in normal production.

　　What is the total relevant cost of raw material Z to the contract?

　　A　$15,336

　　B　$15,400

　　C　$16,200

　　D　$17,496

37 X Ltd manufactures a product called the 'ZT'. The budget for next year was:

Annual sales	10,000 units
	$ per unit
Selling price	20
Variable cost	14
Fixed costs	3
Profit	3

　　If the selling price of the ZT were reduced by 10 per cent, the sales revenue that would be needed to generate the original budgeted profit would be

　　A　$270,000

　　B　$180,000

　　C　$200,000

　　D　$250,000

PAPER C01 : FUNDAMENTALS OF MANAGEMENT ACCOUNTING

38 A company is faced with a shortage of skilled labour next period.

When determining the production plan that will maximise the company's profit next period, the company's products should be ranked according to their:

- A profit per hour of skilled labour
- B profit per unit of product sold
- C contribution per hour of skilled labour
- D contribution per unit of product sold

39 Which of the following would contribute towards a favourable sales price variance (tick all that apply)?

- (a) The standard sales price per unit was set too high
- (b) Price competition in the market was not as fierce as expected
- (c) Sales volume was higher than budgeted and therefore sales revenue was higher than budgeted

40 Which of the following is a benefit of locating management accounting within the individual business unit?

- A Cost saving
- B Adoption of best practice
- C Closer to the business needs
- D Consistency of approach across the organisation

41 The following data relate to a process for the latest period.

Opening work in progress	300 kg valued as follows
	Input material $1,000
	Conversion cost $200
Input during period	8,000 kg at a cost of $29,475
Conversion costs	$11,977
Output	7,000 kg
Closing work in progress	400 kg

Closing work in progress is complete as to input materials and 70 per cent complete as to conversion costs.

Losses are expected to be 10 per cent of input during the period and they occur at the end of the process. Losses have a scrap value of $2 per kg.

The value of the completed output (to the nearest $) is $....................

MOCK ASSESSMENT 1 QUESTIONS : SECTION 5

42 R Ltd absorbs overheads based on units produced. In one period 110,000 units were produced and the actual overheads were $500,000. Overheads were $50,000 over-absorbed in the period.

The overhead absorption rate was $ _____ per unit.

43 Budgetary control statements are required by statute.

True or false?

44 Consider the following statements about Net Present Value (NPV)

(i) Takes account of the time value of money

(ii) Considers how quickly the project will pay back the initial investment

(iii) Uses cash flows

(iv) It is an absolute measure

Which of the statements are true?

A (i) and (iii) only

B (ii), (iii) and (iv) only

C All of them

D (i), (ii) and (iii) only

Questions 45 and 46 are based on the following data

The total figures from TY Division's budgetary control report are as follows.

	Fixed budget	Flexed budget allowances	Actual results
	$	$	$
Total sales revenue	520,000	447,000	466,500
Total variable cost	389,000	348,000	329,400
Total contribution	131,000	99,000	137,100

45 (a) The sales price variance for the period is $.................... adverse/favourable

(b) The sales volume contribution variance for the period is $.................... adverse/favourable

46 (a) The total expenditure variance for the period is $.................... adverse/favourable

(b) The total budget variance for the period is $.................... adverse/favourable

165

PAPER C01 : FUNDAMENTALS OF MANAGEMENT ACCOUNTING

47 **In process costing, if an abnormal loss arises, the process account is generally:**

- A debited with the scrap value of the abnormal loss units
- B debited with the full production cost of the abnormal loss units
- C credited with the scrap value of the abnormal loss units
- D credited with the full production cost of the abnormal loss units

48 **The Drop In Cafe sells specialist coffees to customers to drink on the premises or to take away.**

The proprietors have established that the cost of ingredients is a wholly variable cost in relation to the number of cups of coffee sold whereas staff costs are semi-variable and rent costs are fixed.

Within the relevant range, as the number of cups of coffee sold increases (delete as appropriate):

(a) The ingredients cost per cup sold will increase/decrease/stay the same.

(b) The staff cost per cup sold will increase/decrease/stay the same.

(c) The rent cost per cup sold will increase/decrease/stay the same.

49 **H Limited budgets to produce and sell 4,000 units of product H next year. The amount of capital investment required to support product H will be $290,000 and H Limited requires a rate of return of 14 per cent on all capital invested.**

The full cost per unit of product H is $45.90.

To the nearest penny, the selling price per unit of product H that will achieve the specified return on investment is

- A $52.33
- B $54.96
- C $56.05
- D $53.37

50 **Which of the following are features of the service industry?**

(i) Intangibility

(ii) Heterogeneity

(iii) Simultaneous production and consumption

(iv) Perishability

- A (i) only
- B (i) and (ii)
- C (i), (ii) and (iii)
- D (i), (ii), (iii) and (iv)

Section 6

MOCK ASSESSMENT 2

1   Which of the following could not be classified as a cost unit?

   A   Ream of paper

   B   Barrel of beer

   C   Chargeable man-hour

   D   Hospital

2   There are three departments in a factory.

   Department A occupies 2,000 sq. metres

   Department B occupies 2,500 sq. metres

   Department C occupies 500 sq. metres

   Annual rent = $40,000

   The combined rent apportioned to Department A and B is

   A $16,000

   B $20,000

   C $24,000

   D $36,000

3   Which of the following could be a step fixed cost?

   A   Direct material cost

   B   Electricity cost to operate a packing machine

   C   Depreciation cost of the packing machine

   D   Depreciation cost of all packing machines in the factory

4   Which of the following is not one of the main purposes of management accounting?

   A   Planning

   B   Reporting

   C   Decision Making

   D   Controlling

PAPER C01 : FUNDAMENTALS OF MANAGEMENT ACCOUNTING

5 **Which of the following could be carried out by higher level management?**

(i) Making short term decisions

(ii) Defining the objectives of the business

(iii) Making long run decisions

A   (i), (ii) and (iii)

B   (i) and (ii) only

C   (i) and (iii) only

D   (ii) and (iii) only

6 **The principal budget factor is**

A   The highest value item of cost

B   A factor common to all budget centres

C   The limiting factor

D   A factor known by the budget centre manager

7 **Which of the following are criticisms of standard costing?**

(i) Standard costing was developed when the business environment was stable

(ii) Performance to standard used to be deemed to be satisfactory but today companies are seeking constant improvement

(iii) Emphasis on labour variances is no longer appropriate with the increasing use of automated production techniques

A   (i) and (ii)

B   (i) and (iii)

C   (ii) and (iii)

D   (i), (ii) and (iii)

The following information relates to questions 8–10.

A product is manufactured as a result of two processes, 1 and 2. Details of process 2 for the latest period were as follows:

Materials transferred from process 1	10,000 kg valued at $40,800
Labour and overhead costs	$8,424
Output transferred to finished goods	8,000 kg
Closing work-in-progress	900 kg

Normal loss is 10% of input and losses have a scrap value of $0.30 per kg.

Closing work-in-progress is 100% complete for material, and 75% complete for labour and overheads.

8 The value of the output for the period was $ _____ (to the nearest $).

9 The value of abnormal loss for the period was $ _____ (to the nearest $).

10 The value of the closing work-in-progress for the period was $ _____ (to the nearest $).

11 A company budgets to sell the following number of units of product X.

	January	February	March
Sales units	500	560	590

Inventory of product X at the end of each month is budgeted to be 20 per cent of the number of units required for the following month's sales.

Budgeted production of product X during February is _____ units.

12 Of the four costs shown below, which one would not be included in the cash budget of a greengrocer?

    A   Petrol for the van

    B   Depreciation of the van

    C   Shop assistants wages

    D   Payments made to suppliers

Questions 13 and 14 are based on the following data:

Extracts from Company A's records for July:

The standard cost for a single product during July shows the standard direct material content to be 4 litres at $3 per litre.

Actual results were as follows:

Production   1,250

Materials used   5,100 litres @ $15,500

All materials were purchased and used during the same period.

13 The material price variance for the period was:

    A $500 F

    B $500 A

    C $200 F

    D $200 A

14 The material usage for the period was:

    A $500 F

    B $500 A

    C $300 F

    D $300 A

PAPER C01 : FUNDAMENTALS OF MANAGEMENT ACCOUNTING

15 Which of the following are prime costs?

(i) Direct materials

(ii) Direct labour

(iii) Indirect labour

(iv) Indirect expenses

A (i) and (ii)

B (i) and (iii)

C (ii) and (iii)

D (ii) and (iv)

16 The use of Shared Services Centres (SSCs) can lower the cost of the finance function

Is this statement True or False?

17 The information below shows the number of calls made and the monthly telephone bill for the first quarter of the latest year:

Month	No. of calls	Cost
January	400	$1,050
February	600	$1,700
March	900	$2,300

Using the high–low method the costs could be subdivided into:

A Fixed cost $50   Variable cost per call $2.50

B Fixed cost $50   Variable cost per call $25

C Fixed cost $25   Variable cost per call $2.50

D Fixed cost $25   Variable cost per call $25

18 A company absorbs overheads on standard machine hours which were budgeted at 11,250 with overheads of $258,750. Actual results were 10,980 standard machine hours with overheads of $254,692.

Overheads were:

A under-absorbed by $2,152

B over-absorbed by $4,058

C under-absorbed by $4,058

D over-absorbed by $2,152

19 A project requires an investment of $500,000. It is expected that it will generate cash inflows of $150,000 per year for the next 5 years.

The payback period for the project is _____ years _____ months. (to the nearest month)

20 Which of the following is a possible cause of an adverse labour efficiency variance?

    A   The original standard time was set too high

    B   The employees were more skilled than had been planned for in the standard

    C   Production volume was lower than budgeted

    D   An ideal standard was used for labour time

21 **A flexible budget is**

    A   A budget of variable production costs only

    B   A budget which is updated with actual costs and revenues as they occur during the budget period

    C   A budget which shows the costs and revenues at different levels of activity

    D   A budget which is prepared for a period of six months and reviewed monthly

Following such a review, a further one month's budget is prepared.

22 **An engineering company has been offered the opportunity to bid for a contract which requires a special component.**

Currently, the company has a component in stock, which has a net book value of $250. This component could be used in the contract, but would require modification at a cost of $50. There is no other foreseeable use for the component held in stock. Alternatively, the company could purchase a new specialist component for $280.

The relevant cost of using the component held in stock for this contract is $_____.

Questions 23–25 are based on the following information:

A company manufactures a single product which has the following cost structure based on a production and sales budget of 10,000 units.

	$
Direct materials (4 kg at $3 per kg)	12
Direct labour hours (5 hours at $7 per hour)	35

Variable overheads are incurred at $8 per direct labour hour.

Other costs include

	$
Fixed production overheads	120,000
Selling and distribution overheads	160,000
Fixed administration overheads	80,000

The selling and distribution overheads include a variable element due to a distribution cost of $2 per unit. Selling price is $129 per unit.

PAPER C01 : FUNDAMENTALS OF MANAGEMENT ACCOUNTING

23 How many units must be sold for the company to break even?

    A   8,500
    B   9,000
    C   9,500
    D   1,000

24 The level of revenue which would give a net profit of $40,000 is

    A $1,000,000
    B $1,225,500
    C $1,300,250
    D $1,325,000

25 The margin of safety is

    A   1,000 units
    B   1,250 units
    C   1,440 units
    D   1,500 units

26 If both the selling price and the variable cost per unit of a product rise by 20%, the break-even point will

    A   Remain constant
    B   Increase
    C   Decrease
    D   Impossible to determine

27 During the latest period the number of labour hours worked was 1,000. The wages paid amounted to $14,500 and the labour rate variance was $1,300 adverse. The standard labour rate per hour was:

    A $11.15
    B $13.20
    C $14.50
    D $15.80

28 In January a company produced 1,200 units at a cost of $9,800. In February they produced 1,000 units at a cost of $8,700.

If March production is expected to be 1,250 units, what should be the budgeted cost?

- A $10,000
- B $10,025
- C $10,075
- D $11,025

29 For a company operating a fleet of delivery vehicles, which of the following would be most useful?

- A   Cost per mile
- B   Cost per driver hour
- C   Cost per tonne mile
- D   Cost per tonne carried

30 A firm operates an integrated cost and financial accounting system. The accounting entries for an issue of direct materials to production would be:

- A   DR WIP control account
     CR stores control account
- B   DR finished goods account
     CR stores control account
- C   DR stores control account
     CR WIP control account
- D   DR cost of sales account
     CR WIP control account

31 Which of the following will normally be included in a standard cost card?

- (i)   Direct materials
- (ii)   Direct wages
- (iii) Variable overhead
- (iv)   Fixed overhead

- A   (i) only
- B   (i) and (ii)
- C   (i), (ii) and (iii)
- D   (i), (ii), (iii) and (iv)

32 B — (i) and (ii)

33 A — Production overhead control account

34 A — A 2,500, B 200, C 2,000

35 C — $592

MOCK ASSESSMENT 2 QUESTIONS : SECTION 6

36 Which of the following are objectives of budgeting?

(i) Resource allocation

(ii) Expansion

(iii) Communication

(iv) Co-ordination

A (i), (ii)

B (i), (ii), (iii)

C (i), (iii), (iv)

D (i), (ii), (iii), (iv)

37 Management accounting is required by law

Is the above statement True or False?

38 A method of accounting for overheads involves attributing them to cost units using predetermined rates. This is known as

A overhead allocation

B overhead apportionment

C overhead absorption

D overhead analysis

39 Which of the following would be classified as indirect labour?

A Assembly workers in a car plant

B Bricklayers in a building company

C Store assistants in a factory

D An auditor in a firm of accountants

40 Standards which can be attained under the most favourable conditions, with no allowance for idle time or losses are known as:

A Basic

B Ideal

C Attainable

D Current

41 The difference between the flexed budget and the actual results is known as the:

A Volume variance

B Expenditure variance

C Price variance

D Capacity variance

175

42 A company manufactures a range of products, including product G for which the total cost is $32 per unit. The company's budgeted total cost for the period is $580,000 and the budgeted rate of return on the capital employed of $435,000 is 20%.

The cost-plus selling price of one unit of product G should be (to the nearest cent) $ _____ .

43 ABX are considering purchasing a new machine. The cost of the machine is $75,000. It is expected that the incremental cash flow from the expansion over the next 4 years will be as follows:

Year 1: $5,000

Year 2: $20,000

Year 3: $30,000

Year 4: $10,000

The machine will be sold at the end of the project for $15,000. The above figures include a depreciation charge of $15,000 per year. The company uses a 10% discount rate.

The NPV for the project will be:

- A $70,495
- B $33,205
- C $80,740
- D $22,960

44 Which of the following comments regarding CIMA is incorrect?

- A CIMA are committed to upholding the highest ethical and professional standards
- B CIMA can provide students and members with guidance on how to handle situations where their ethics may be compromised
- C CIMA focuses on organisations in the private sector
- D CIMA is the world's largest and leading professional body of management accountants. Members and students are located in over 160 countries

45 Which of the following items would appear on a job cost sheet?

- (i) materials purchased specifically for the job
- (ii) materials drawn from inventory
- (iii) direct wages
- (iv) direct expenses

- A (i) and (ii)
- B (iii) and (iv)
- C (i), (ii) and (iii)
- D (i), (ii), (iii) and (iv)

MOCK ASSESSMENT 2 QUESTIONS : SECTION 6

46 Which of the following would not be classified as a cost centre in a hotel?

A   Restaurant

B   Rooms

C   Bar

D   Meals served

47 A company has four production departments. Fixed overhead costs are as follows:

Department	$	Hours taken
A	10,000	5
B	5,000	5
C	4,000	4
D	6,000	3

The company produces one product and the time spent in each department is shown above. If overhead is recovered on the basis of labour hours and budgeted production is 2,000 units, the fixed overhead cost per unit is

A $3

B $12

C $12.50

D $17.50

48 The selling price is $100, gross profit is 50%. Which one of the following statements is true?

A   Mark up is 50%

B   Mark up is 100%

C   Mark up is 150%

D   Mark up is impossible to determine without knowing unit cost

49 What are the three objectives of accounting for overhead costs?

(i)   To identify costs in relation to output products or services

(ii) To identify costs in relation to activities and divisions of the organisation

(iii) To identify and control overhead costs

(iv) To identify and control direct costs

A   (i) and (ii)

B   (i), (ii) and (iii)

C   (i), (ii) and (iv)

D   (i), (ii), (iii) and (iv)

50 **Budgeted overhead** = **$100,000**

Actual overhead = $90,000

Budgeted labour hours = 20,000

Actual labour hours = 21,000

Calculate the amount of under/over absorption of overheads.

A   Over absorption $15,000

B   Over absorption $5,000

C   Under absorption $15,000

D   Under absorption $5,000

Section 7

ANSWERS TO MOCK ASSESSMENT 1

1 B

Cleaner in a cleaning company.

The cleaner's wages can be identified with a specific cost unit therefore this is a direct cost. The wages paid to the other three people cannot be identified with specific cost units. Therefore they would be indirect costs.

2 A

The principal budget factor is the factor which limits the activities of the organisation at is often the starting point in budget preparation.

3 FALSE

Management accounting is used by internal management, it is usually not available to external parties. Financial accounting is used by shareholders.

4 D

Finished goods inventory account.

5 Overheads for the period were over-absorbed by $95,000.

Workings:

Overhead absorption rate = $1,250,000/250,000 = $5 per hour

	$
Absorbed overhead = 220,000 hours × $5	1,100,000
Actual overhead incurred	1,005,000
Over-absorbed overhead	95,000

PAPER C01 : FUNDAMENTALS OF MANAGEMENT ACCOUNTING

6 Income statement

	Debit	Credit	No entry in this account
Production overhead account		✓	
Work in progress account			✓
Income statement	✓		

7 C

Year	Cash flow	Cumulative cash flow
	$000	$000
0	(1,200)	(1,200)
1	240	(960)
2	265	(695)
3	240	(455)
4	660	205
5	290	495

Payback is achieved between years 3 and 4.

Payback is 3 years plus (455/660 × 12) months = 3 years 8 months.

This is less than the target payback period of 4 years, therefore the investment should be undertaken.

8 After the apportionment of the service department costs, the total overhead cost of the production departments will be (to the nearest $000):

Machining	$230,000
Finishing	$190,000

Workings:

	Machining	Finishing	Stores	Maintenance
	$000	$000	$000	$000
Apportioned costs	190.00	175.00	30.0	25.0
Stores apportionment	18.00	9.00	(30.0)	3.0
Maintenance apportionment	21.00	5.60	1.4	(28.0)
Stores apportionment	0.84	0.42	(1.4)	0.14
Maintenance apportionment	0.11	0.03	–	(0.14)
Total	229.95	190.05		

MOCK ASSESSMENT 1 ANSWERS : SECTION 7

9 C

The actual contribution earned by R Limited last month was $31,360.

$(32,000 – 800 – 880 + 822 + 129 + 89) = $31,360.

10 B

The period fixed cost is $3,000 (where the line crosses the y axis)

The variable cost per meal delivered is $5

Workings:

Variable cost per meal = ($5,000 – $3,000) ÷ 400 MEALS = 5

11 D

Information for strategic management tends to be summarised and information for operational management tends to be provided frequently

12 Solution:

Year	Cash flow ($)	Discount factor (7%)	Present value (future value x discount factor)
0	(450,000)	1	(450,000)
1	120,000	0.935	112,200
2	150,000	0.873	130,950
3	160,000	0.816	130,560
4	120,000	0.763	91,560
		NPV =	15,270

This project has a positive NPV of $15,270

13 The budgeted production overhead absorption rate for the Assembly Department will be $1.30 per unit.

Workings:

	Assembly $
Budgeted overheads	100,000
Reapportioned stores overhead 60% × $50,000	30,000
Total budgeted overhead	130,000
Budgeted output	100,000

$$OAR = \frac{\$130,000}{100,000}$$

= $1.30 per unit

14 The overheads for the Finishing Department were *over-absorbed by $40,000*.

Workings:

	Finishing
	$
Budgeted overheads	150,000
Reapportioned stores overhead 40% × $50,000	20,000
Total budgeted overhead	170,000
Budgeted output	100,000

$$\text{OAR} = \frac{\$170,000}{100,000}$$

= $1.70 per unit

	$
Absorbed overhead $1.70 × 100,000	170,000
Actual overhead incurred	130,000
Over absorption	40,000

15 D

The company quote for the job should be $250.

Workings:

	Job quote
	$
Variable production costs	125
Fixed production overheads ($250,000 ÷ 12,500) × 3	60
Selling, distribution and administration	15
Total cost	200
Profit margin 20%	50
Quote	250

16 Depreciation and provisions for doubtful debts are not cash flows and would not be included in a cash budget.

MOCK ASSESSMENT 1 ANSWERS : SECTION 7

17 The production budget for month 1 will be 6,600 units.

Workings:

	Month 1 Units	Month 2 Units	Month 3 Units	Month 4 Units
Sales	6,000	7,000	5,500	6,000
Production				
40% in the month	2,400	2,800	2,200	2,400
60% in the previous month	4,200	3,300	3,600	
Production	6,600	6,100	5,800	

18 The material cost budget for Month 2 will be $30,500.

Workings:

Month 2   6,100 units produced @ $5 per unit = $30,500.

19 A

The quantity to be purchased equals material usage + materials closing inventory − materials opening inventory

20 B

The overhead budget for an activity level of 80% would be $115,000.

Workings:

Using the high/low method

		$	
High	75%	112,500	
Low	50%	100,000	
Change	25%	12,500	– variable cost of 25%
	1%	500	– variable cost of 1%

Substitute into 75% activity	$
Total overhead	112,500
Variable cost element 75 × $500	37,500
Fixed cost element	75,000

Total overhead for 80% activity	
Variable cost element 80 × $500	40,000
Fixed cost element	75,000
Total overhead	115,000

PAPER C01 : FUNDAMENTALS OF MANAGEMENT ACCOUNTING

21 The correct answers are:

- repayment of a bank loan
- proceeds from the sale of a non-current asset.

Both these items result in a cash flow and would therefore be included in the cash budget. However, they would not be included in the income statement. The bad debts write off would be included in the income statement, but not in the cash budget.

22 B

The graph is known as a conventional breakeven chart.

23 The amount budgeted to be paid to suppliers in September is $289,000.

Workings:

	July $	August $	September $
Purchases	250,000	300,000	280,000
25% paid in the month of purchase	62,500	75,000	70,000
5% discount allowed	(3,125)	(3,750)	(3,500)
70% paid in the first month		175,000	210,000
5% paid in the second month			12,500
Budgeted payment			289,000

24 B

The difference in the values ($) between point X and point Y on the profit volume chart represents *profit*.

25 A

The shaded area on the breakeven chart represents *loss*.

26

	Debit	Credit	No entry in this account
Material usage variance account	✓		
Raw material control account			✓
Work-in-progress account		✓	

184

MOCK ASSESSMENT 1 ANSWERS : SECTION 7

27 The cost of the abnormal loss is $460.

Workings:

	$
Direct material cost	26,000
Labour cost	12,000
Production overhead cost	5,700
	43,700

	Kg
Input	20,000
Normal loss	1,000
Expected output	19,000
Actual output	18,800
Abnormal loss	200

Cost per kg = $43,700/19,000 = $2.30

Cost of abnormal loss = $2.30 × 200 kg = $460.

28 D

The relevant cost of labour is $5,500

		$
Skilled labour: basic pay	(250 × $10)	2,500
Skilled labour: contribution forgone	(250 × $12)	3,000
Unskilled labour – will be paid anyway		0
		5,500

Contribution is measured after deducting the basic labour cost, so the relevant cost of the scarce skilled labour is the basic pay plus the contribution obtainable from doing the other work.

29 (i), (ii) and (iii) are relevant costs. (iv) sunk costs is not considered relevant as any decision taken will not alter that cost.

30 A

- A budget would be prepared by a management accountant. The income statement, statement of financial position (balance sheet) and cash flow statement all form part of the annual statutory accounts prepared by financial accountants.

PAPER C01 : FUNDAMENTALS OF MANAGEMENT ACCOUNTING

31 A

Materials price variance:

	$
26,400 × $13 =	343,200
Actual	336,600
Favourable	$6,600

Materials usage variance:

		$
Should have used:	12,000 × 2 × $13	= 312,000
Did use	26,400 × $13	= 343,200
		$31,200 Adverse.

32 A

Labour rate:

	$
40,200 × $4	160,800
Actual	168,840
Adverse	$8,040

Labour efficiency:

		$
Should have taken:	12,000 × 3.3 × $4	= 158,400
Did take:	40,200 × $4	= 160,800
		$2,400 Adverse

33 The sales price variance for the period was $69,000 adverse

46,000 units should sell for (× $34)	1,564,000
But did sell for	1,495,000
Sales price variance	69,000 adverse

34 The sales volume contribution variance for the period was $14,000 favourable

	Units
Budgeted sales volume	45,000
Actual sales volume	46,000
Sales volume variance in units	1,000 favourable
× standard contribution per unit	$14
Sales volume contribution variance	$14,000 favourable

MOCK ASSESSMENT 1 ANSWERS : SECTION 7

35 B

Characteristics of Service Costing:

(i) High levels of indirect costs as a proportion of total costs, e.g. rent for a restaurant. YES

(ii) Use of composite cost units, e.g. tonne mile. YES

(iii) Use of equivalent units. This is used in process costing. NO

So B – (i) and (ii).

36 C

Relevant cost of a regularly used material in inventory is its replacement cost (600 × $27) = $16,200

37 A

The sales revenue that would be needed to generate the original budgeted profit would be $270,000.

Workings:

Fixed costs are not relevant because they will remain unaltered.

Original budgeted contribution = 10,000 units × $(20 – 14) = $60,000

Revised contribution per unit = $(18 — 14) = $4

Required number of units to achieve same contribution = $60,000/$4 = 15,000 units

Required sales revenue — 15,000 units × $18 revised price — $270,000

38 C

When determining the production plan that will maximise the company's profit next period, the company's products should be ranked according to their contribution per hour of skilled labour.

39 Only reason (b) would contribute to a favourable sales price variance.

Reason (a) would result in an adverse variance.

Reason (c) would not necessarily result in any sales price variance because all the units could have been sold at standard price.

40 C

Being closer to the business needs is an advantage of having the management accounting located within the business unit. A, B and C are benefits from shared services centres (SSCs) or business process outsourcing (BPO)

PAPER C01 : FUNDAMENTALS OF MANAGEMENT ACCOUNTING

41 The value of the completed output is $38,500

Workings:

| | | | | | Equivalent kg | |
					Input material	Conversion costs
Input	kg	Output	kg			
Opening WIP	300	Finished output	7,000		7,000	7,000
Input	8,000	Normal loss	800		–	–
		Abnormal loss	100		100	100
		Closing WIP	400		400 70%	280
	8,300		8,300		7,500	7,380

	$	$	$
Costs			
Opening WIP	1,200	1,000	200
Period costs	41,452	29,475	11,977
Normal loss	(1,600)	(1,600)	–
	41,052	28,875	12,177
Cost per equivalent kg	5.50	3.85	1.65

The value of the completed output is $5.50 × 7,000 kg = $38,500

42 The overhead absorption rate was $5 per unit.

Workings:

	$
Actual overheads	500,000
Over absorption	50,000
Overhead absorbed	550,000

Overhead absorption rate = $550,000/110,000 units = $5.

43 FALSE

There is no statutory requirement for companies to produce budgetary control statements

44 D

(ii) relates to the payback method.

45 (a) The sales price variance is $(466,500 – 447,000) = $19,500 favourable

(b) The sales volume contribution variance is $(99,000 – 131,000) = $32,000 adverse

MOCK ASSESSMENT 1 ANSWERS : SECTION 7

46 (a) The total expenditure variance is $(329,400 − 348,000) = $18,600 favourable

(b) The total budget variance is $(137,100 − 131,000) = $6,100 favourable

47 D

The process account is credited with the full production cost of the abnormal loss, and the abnormal loss account is debited.

48 Within the relevant range, as the number of cups of coffee sold increases:

(a) the ingredients cost per cup sold will stay the same.

(b) the staff cost per cup sold will decrease.

(c) the rent cost per cup sold will decrease.

49 C

The selling price per unit of product H that will achieve the specified return on investment is $56.05

Workings:

Required return from capital invested to support product H = $290,000 × 14%

= $40,600

Required return per unit of product H sold = $40,600/4,000 = $10.15

Required selling price = $45.90 full cost + $10.15 = $56.05

50 D

INTANGIBILITY – Output takes the form of a performance, e.g. a waiter.

HETEROGENEITY – Standard of service is variable due to human element, e.g. chef.

SIMULTANEOUS PRODUCTION CONSUMPTION – e.g. hairdresser.

PERISHABILITY – Cannot hold stock, e.g. airline seats.

So all are features – Answer D.

Section 8

ANSWERS TO MOCK ASSESSMENT 2

1   D

Alternatives A, B and C are all examples of cost units. A hospital might be classified as a cost centre.

2   D

Rent Department A = $\dfrac{2,000}{5,000}$ × $40,000 = $16,000

Rent Department B = $\dfrac{2,500}{5,000}$ × $40,000 = $20,000

So Department A + Department B = $16,000 + $20,000
= $36,000

3   D

Cost D could behave in a step fashion over a period of time. The total depreciation cost would remain fixed for a certain number of machines. If an additional machine is required the total cost will increase to a higher level at which it will again remain constant. The addition of further machines will increase the total depreciation cost in successive steps. Cost A is a variable cost, cost B is a semi-variable cost and cost C is a fixed cost.

4   B

Reporting is the main purpose of financial accounting.

5   A

Higher-level management could be involved with all levels of decision-making within an enterprise, in short-term decisions as well as longer-term decisions.

6   C

The principal budget factor is the limiting factor.

7   D

PAPER C01 : FUNDAMENTALS OF MANAGEMENT ACCOUNTING

8 STEP 1:

STATEMENT OF EQUIVALENT UNITS

	Total units		Materials units		Labour & overhead units
Completed output	8,000	(100%)	8,000	(100%)	8,000
Normal loss	1,000	(0%)	–	(0%)	
Abnormal loss	100	(100%)	100	(100%)	100
Closing WIP	900	(100%)	900	(75%)	675
	10,000		9,000		8,775

STEP 2:

STATEMENT OF COST PER EQUIVALENT UNIT

	Materials	Labour & overhead
Total costs	*$40,500	$8,424
Equivalent units	9,000	8,775
Cost per equivalent unit	$4.50	$0.96

*$40,800 less scrap value normal loss $300 = $40,500

Total cost per unit = $(4.50 + 0.96)

= $5.46

STATEMENT OF EVALUATION

Output

8,000 kg @ $5.46 = $43,680.

9 The value of abnormal loss for the period was $546 (to the nearest $)

From question 33, 100 units abnormal loss × $5.46 = $546.

10 The value of the closing work-in-progress for the period was $4,698 (to the nearest $)

From question 33, costs per equivalent unit are:
Materials $4.50
Labour and Overhead $0.96

Evaluation of work-in-progress:

	$
Materials 900 equivalent units × $4.50	4,050
Labour and Overhead 675 equivalent units × $0.96	648
	4,698

MOCK ASSESSMENT 2 ANSWERS : SECTION 8

11   Budgeted production of product X during February is 566 units.

	Units
Required for budgeted sales	560
Plus closing inventory (20% × 590 units)	118
	678
Less opening inventory (20% × 560 units)	(112)
Budgeted production volume	566

12   B

Petrol, wages and payments made to suppliers could all appear on a cash budget. Odd one out is depreciation, where no cash changes hands.

13   D

The material price variance for the period was:

5,100 litres did cost	$15,500
5,100 litres should have cost	$15,300
	$200 A

14   D

The material usage for the period was:

1,250 units should have used	5,000 litres
Did use	5,100 litres
Usage variance in litres	100 A litres
X standard price (× $3)	$300 A

15   A

Prime costs consist of direct materials, direct labour and direct expenses.

16   True

The use of SSCs brings the whole finance function together, therefore enjoying economies of scale and avoiding duplication. It will therefore result in lower operating costs.

PAPER C01 : FUNDAMENTALS OF MANAGEMENT ACCOUNTING

17 A

	Calls	Cost
Highest	900	$2,300
Lowest	400	$1,050
	500	$1,250

Variable cost $= \dfrac{\$1{,}250}{500} = \$2.50$ per call

Fixed cost = Total cost − variable cost

$= \$1{,}050 - (400 \times \$2.50)$

$= \$1{,}050 - \$1{,}000$

$= \$50$

So fixed cost = $50 and variable cost = $2.50 per call.

18 A

Overhead absorption rate $= \dfrac{\$258{,}750}{11{,}250} = \$23$ per standard machine hour

	$
Overhead absorbed = 10,980 std. hours × $23	252,540
Overhead incurred	254,692
Under absorption	2,152

19 $500,000/$150,000 = 3 years + (0.33 × 12) months

= 3 years 4 months.

20 D

An ideal standard makes no allowances for stoppages or idle time therefore it is most likely to result in an adverse labour efficiency variance.

If the original standard time was set too high then the labour efficiency variance would be favourable. Employees who are more skilled are likely to work faster than standard, again resulting in a favourable efficiency variance. The efficiency variance is based on the expected time for the actual production volume therefore it is not affected by a difference between budgeted and actual production volume.

21 C

A flexible budget is one which shows the costs and revenues at different levels of activity.

MOCK ASSESSMENT 2 ANSWERS : SECTION 8

22 The relevant cost of the component in stock is $50.

The company has no other use for the component. It would cost $50 to modify. Alternatively, the company could buy a new component for $280. It is cheaper to modify the existing component, and the relevant cost (i.e. the future cash flow arising as a consequence of using the component) is the cost of modification.

	$
Total variable cost	
Materials (4 kg at $3 per kg)	12
Direct labour hours (5 hours at $7 per hour)	35
Variable overheads (5 hours at $8 per hour)	40
Distribution	2
	89

23 **A**

	$
Selling price	129
Variable cost	89
Contribution per unit	40

Fixed costs	$
Fixed overheads	120,000
Selling and distribution	140,000
Administration	80,000
	340,000

$$= \frac{£340,000}{£40} = 8,500 \text{ units}$$

24 **B**

	$
Total fixed costs	340,000
Profits required	40,000
Required contribution	380,000

$$= \frac{\$380,000}{£40} = 9,500 \text{ units}$$

Revenue = 9,500 × $129 = $1,225,500.

PAPER C01 : FUNDAMENTALS OF MANAGEMENT ACCOUNTING

25 D

	Units
Budgeted production and sales	10,000
Break-even sales	8,500
Margin of safety	1,500

26 C

Assuming selling price is above variable cost, contribution per unit will rise so fewer units need to be sold so break-even will fall.

27 B

Wages paid	$14,500
Rate variance	$1,300 (A)
Standard rate for hours worked	$13,200

Standard rate per hour = $13,200/1,000 = $13.20.

28 C

Production units	1,200	1,000
Cost	$9,800	$8,700
Difference per 200 units	$1,100	
Difference per 50 units	$275	

So $9,800 + 275 = $10,075.

29 C

The most useful measure would be cost per tonne mile since it measures both distance and amount carried.

30 A

The entry would be DR work-in-progress control account and CR stores control account.

31 D

Direct Materials, Direct Wages, Variable Overhead and Fixed Overhead are all included in a standard cost card.

32 B

Alternatives (i) and (ii) are valid equivalent units as used in process costing.

33 A

This is known as Production overhead control account.

34 A

Limiting factor labour hours

Contribution per limiting factor

	A	B	C
	$30	$15	$20
Rank	1	3	2

	Units	Hours
Product A	2,500	2,500
Product C	2,000	3,000
Product B	200	600
		6,100

35 C

	$
March sales (15% × $400)	60
February sales (35% × $800)	280
January sales (42% × $600)	252
	592

36 C

Resource allocation, communication and co-ordination are all objectives of budgeting, odd one out is expansion.

37 False

Financial accounting is required by law, but management accounting is not.

38 C

Overhead allocation is the allotment of whole items of cost to cost units or cost centres. Overhead apportionment is the sharing out of costs over a number of cost centres according to the benefit used. Overhead analysis refers to the whole process of recording and accounting for overheads.

PAPER C01 : FUNDAMENTALS OF MANAGEMENT ACCOUNTING

39 C

Alternatives A, B and C are all direct labour. A stores assistant is an example of indirect labour.

40 B

Standards which can be attained under the most favourable conditions, with no allowance for idle time or losses are known as ideal standards.

41 B

The difference between the flexed budget and the actual results is known as the expenditure variance.

42 Required annual profit = $435,000 × 20% = $87,000

Profit as a percentage of total cost = $87,000/$580,000 = 15%

Required cost-plus selling price = $32 + (15% × $32) = **$36.80**

43 B

Year	Cash flow ($)	Discount factor (10%)	Present value
0	(75,000)	1	(75,000)
1	20,000	0.909	18,180
2	35,000	0.826	28,910
3	45,000	0.751	33,795
4	25,000 + 15,000 = 40,000	0.683	27,320
		NPV =	**33,205**

44 C

CIMA supports organisations in both the private and public sector. It focuses on the needs of businesses, no matter what type of business

45 D

Materials purchased specifically for the job, or drawn from inventory, direct wages and direct materials would all be shown on a job cost sheet.

46 D

This question relates to costs in a hotel. Alternatives A, B and C are all department or cost centres. A meal served would be a cost unit.

47 C

Total fixed overhead cost	= $10,000 + $5,000 + $4,000 + $6,000
	= $25,000
Budgeted production	= 2,000 units
Fixed overhead cost per unit	= $\dfrac{\$25,000}{2,000}$
	= $12.50

48 B

If gross profit is 50%, unit cost is 50% of the sales price. If unit cost is $50 and selling price is $100, then it has been marked up by a factor of 100%.

49 B

Alternatives (i), (ii) and (iii) are all concerned with overheads. Direct costs are prime costs.

50 A

Budgeted overhead rate per hour = $100,000 ÷ 20,000 = $5

Actual hours × standard rate (21,000 × $5)	= $105,000
Actual overhead	= $90,000
Over absorption	$15,000